HOW TO BE A
SUCCESSFUL
THERAPIST

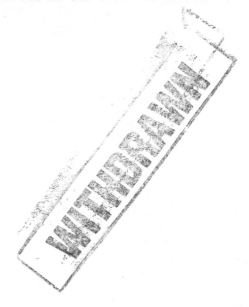

How to be a Successful Therapist
by
Celia Johnson and Helen Parkins

First published in April 2009 by Gold Bridge Publications,
PO Box 1131, Guildford, Surrey, GU1 9LY

Designed by Two Associates
Printed and bound in the UK by CPI Mackays, Chatham ME5 8TD

A catalogue record for this book is available from the British Library

ISBN 978-0-9562314-0-6

HOW TO BE A
SUCCESSFUL
THERAPIST

A GUIDE TO STARTING AND RUNNING
YOUR OWN COMPLEMENTARY
THERAPY BUSINESS

CELIA JOHNSON
AND HELEN PARKINS

PRAISE FOR *HOW TO BE A SUCCESSFUL THERAPIST*

As a professional adviser to therapists, I am often asked questions about business- related matters. There is a need for clear, impartial advice for both the new and experienced practitioner in the complicated business world.

This concise and engaging book contains all that and more. I highly recommend it to any practitioner wanting to become a successful therapist.

Gareth Millard, Director, Three Counties Insurance Brokers Ltd.

A goldmine of clear, practical advice from start to finish: a 'must have' for students and new and established therapists alike.

Sue Hall, Founder, British Kinesiology Centre

This is a most interesting and comprehensive book. There is guidance on most if not all aspects of the business of complementary therapy. The case study input and draft GP letters are very helpful but the check lists provided are particularly useful in bringing together the information and important areas of each section or chapter.

I would recommend the book with confidence for all those venturing into private practice in complementary therapies. It is a lonely and daunting world at the outset, and having such well researched and sound information to hand can only benefit the new therapist. Such areas as advertising, keeping accounts and treating awkward clients are very clearly stated and helpful.

Registering with the Data Protection Act is also covered, as is having a CRB check in place. All the information given is supported by sound advice and includes details of where to contact organisations where a therapist may need to register for a license, a police check or other official organisations.

I have given my opinion as to why this would be a vital piece of literature for the budding therapist but I feel this is also a very important book to be kept on the shelf in the clinic of a well established therapist. As most therapists are self employed or lone therapists it is often easy to fall behind with the latest information and legal requirements, however hard we try. This book will bring you up to date on even the latest information including that of the Independent Safeguarding Authority which is a vital board to register with.

I wish the authors every success and must thank them for producing such a supportive book full of good advice and useful information. I advise therapists in all disciplines to look out for it.

Jennifer Wayte, Vice President, Federation of Holistic Therapists
Education Chair of the General Council for Massage Therapy

Biographies

 Celia Johnson has been a professional musician, a nurse, and for the last twenty years, a massage therapist. After graduating from the Royal College of Music, she joined the Hallé orchestra as a double bass player. Some years later she left the orchestra to train as a nurse. Once qualified, she nursed in most areas of acute care, including Accident and Emergency. She also continued to play the double bass, freelancing with orchestras throughout the UK.

Her time in nursing sparked an interest in complementary therapies, and she trained and qualified firstly in Reflex Zone Therapy, then massage, and Reiki to the level of Master Practitioner.

Finding that complementary therapists rarely seemed to join forces or to share and learn from their working experiences, she soon set up and ran a support group for practitioners in her area. Their many questions sparked the idea of writing the previous edition of this book. Her articles have been published in professional journals such as *Positive Health*, *Massage and Health Review* and the *International Journal of Theatre Nursing* and online for Holisticpro.com. She has given talks on local radio and the BBC.

As well as running a thriving private practice, Celia gives talks and workshops on business skills and also delivers First Aid training. Her wisdom and friendly inclusive approach make her a much sought after speaker and teacher.

Helen Parkins is qualified commercial solicitor turned business advisor. In various guises, she has been advising, training, speaking and writing for nearly twenty years. She is also a qualified MTI and ITEC massage therapist.

The initial driving force behind the 'one-stop shop' team of small business experts, Zestworks, Helen today continues to run her own business advising clients in and around London and the south. She is co-author of *A Zest for Business* and regular contributor to *In Touch* magazine. A popular speaker, with a practical and de-mystifying approach to the law, she is a partner of the British Library's Business and IP Centre, and runs a series of innovative workshops there for small business owners and entrepreneurs. She has also held similar workshops for local authorities.

The rest of her time is spent working with her clients, ranging from those at start-up stage to those with global presence. Known for her warmth and personable style, Helen combines her extensive experience and expertise to help her clients establish enriching, successful businesses for themselves.

Contents

FOREWORD

Over the 27 years that I have been in the beauty industry, I have seen, met and employed some absolutely brilliant therapists. Many of them have had amazing dreams and aspirations of owning their own businesses. However, only a handful of those will truly succeed. Being a fantastic therapist is not enough to automatically secure a successful business and many therapists are left wondering what has caused them to fail. The answer to that, in my opinion, is that they do not recognise that their therapy and good business skills go hand in hand. For example, a therapist might feel guilty about what she charges, or may simply fail to take into account what she needs to pay in tax.

A saying of mine has always been that 'knowledge equals power,' and I believe the power comes from ensuring that you take into account every facet of running your business – from the therapies you plan to administer, your customer service, your promotions and the daily functioning of your business right down to the nitty-gritty details of your accounts and paying taxes. Unfortunately, not all therapists are taught how to run a business.

That's why every therapist needs this book – to help give them the knowledge, confidence and tools they need to become a truly successful therapist. As well as being a great guide for the newly qualified therapist, it can also remind those who are established how to improve and evolve their business to ensure continued success.

I look forward to seeing a boom in the industry with therapists who are not only respected for their work but also for their business acumen.

Bharti Vyas

1 LAYING THE FOUNDATIONS

Whether you think you can or think you can't,
you are probably right

HENRY FORD SNR

What sort of a person are you? Are you single, married, divorced? Do you live alone, share with friends or live with your family? Are you planning to work in a big city, a small town, a tiny village? Is the area affluent or poor? All these factors will influence the kind of practice you could set up.

Bearing in mind your personal life and circumstances, how suited are you to earning your living as a therapist? This may seem a silly question, but you should ask yourself not only will you suit your therapy, but will your therapy suit you?

It goes without saying that you need to be a caring empathetic person and good at whatever therapy or therapies you plan to practise. You also need to be truly professional, absolutely straight in your dealings with clients and colleagues alike. It is likely that you will be self employed, so you'll be taking responsibility for all your dealings with money – deciding what you will charge per treatment, keeping records of what you have earned and spent on your business, planning for 'lean' patches, preparing accounts for the tax man, arranging adequate insurance cover and contributing to a pension.

You must ensure that you comply with legal requirements such as keeping records, health and safety at work, and perhaps storing hazardous substances. If you work from home you may need a licence or to be inspected by your local council. You should regard dealing with formal (legal) requirements as putting the building blocks in place for a successful business. If you're not prepared to deal with the details, then you'll limit your business and the success you could achieve. If you get things wrong, a fine or a court case could cost you several thousand pounds and put you out of business altogether. If you're not confident about managing the legal side of things yourself, seek professional advice. It's much better to be safe than sorry.

You will have to manage your own work load and schedule, and you may have to deal with some difficult and demanding people. You will need to create and maintain good relationships with your own clientele. You are also likely to be dealing with other health professionals and be responsible for arranging your Continuing Professional Development. You will need to develop relationships with other therapists, doctors, suppliers, an accountant and possibly a financial adviser.

If you have previously been in paid employment, all this can be a daunting prospect. But much of this is about having a mindset of being professional. It becomes easier the more you do it.

One of the disadvantages of being a therapist is that it is mostly an isolated occupation, with little opportunity to observe and learn from more experienced therapists. Your clients may not tell you that they didn't like what you did for them – they just won't come back.

If you are to build a successful practice, you'll need a large client base of loyal, satisfied customers who recommend you to all their friends and work colleagues. For that to happen, they'll need to have faith in your treatments, complete confidence in you and know that you will always treat them with respect, courtesy and integrity and work for their highest good.

For this reason you need to look carefully at what you are

offering, how that fits with your life, whether it is realistic and how you will achieve it.

How would your friends describe you?

- a bit flaky?
- completely professional?
- inspiring confidence?
- capable of recognising your limitations?
- good at being your word?

INTEGRITY

Being your word (integrity) is absolutely essential to a being professional. What do I mean by that? I mean, if you say you'll phone someone, you do so. If you offer to look something up for them, you do so. You'll be ready to begin a treatment at the time you arranged, and it will take (roughly) the length of time you told your client. You will charge the amount you discussed with them prior to treatment, and expect them to pay you promptly. The treatment will be done to the very best of your ability, and if their problem is beyond your scope, you will refer them to someone appropriate. In short, you will be taking responsibility for every aspect of your business and your clients' satisfaction. It is essential that you make this investment in your business so that the right things are in place before you begin.

■ Marie is a business woman who, despite her busy schedule, arrives promptly for a facial. Donna is still with her previous client who arrived late and keeps Marie waiting half an hour. Marie values her time more than a facial, however good it is: before she has even had her facial, she decides she will not go to Donna again.

- Peter works as an acupuncturist at a physiotherapy clinic. He often forgets to put appointments in his diary and the clinic has to call him when the patients are waiting and he has not turned up. The clinic receptionist is embarrassed, but Peter cannot understand why he doesn't seem to be able to make a living: the patients prefer to see a more reliable acupuncturist.

- The High Street complementary therapy clinic is having an open day which begins at 10am. I attend at 11.30am and there are no therapists there at all. I bump into some of my own clients, who went there to meet new therapists but as there are none there, ask me for my business card for their friends.

- Sarah is a massage therapist who swaps treatments with Alice, a reflexologist. They agreed between them that Sarah would be the one to keep track of whether one of them owes the other any treatments. One day, Sarah suggests that Alice owes her four treatments. Alice is furious that Sarah has not taken responsibility for keeping track as agreed. Alice spends three hours checking through her own records and finds that neither owes the other anything. She insists they pay one another in future.

All the above examples are of therapists who do not keep their word, and all will find it difficult to earn a decent living from therapy unless they change their behaviour. They may be good therapists but they do not show integrity in their work.

Hygiene and appearance

It should be unnecessary to state the obvious about personal hygiene, but I shall do so anyway. No client wants a lungful of BO as you stretch across them, or your loose hair trailing over their face or your sweat dripping on them. You must take a daily shower or bath, and use a deodorant/anti-perspirant. Daily fresh underwear and work clothes are essential. If you become hot and sweaty when you work, take time to freshen yourself up between seeing clients. A pot of wipes in your bag or treatment room should be sufficient for this.

Nails should be kept clean, short and preferably free of nail polish. Your hair should be tidy and be tied back or put up if necessary. Jewellery is best kept to a minimum for those doing any kind of body work as it could scratch your client and get in your way. The effects of garlic, coffee, and other strong smelling foods should be minimised by regular mouth hygiene. Your clients will not like it if you smell of cigarette smoke, and nor should you use perfume. Keep the latter for your time off. Male therapists should be aware that stubble can look unkempt and unclean. It is preferable to be clean shaven or to have a very neat beard or moustache. If you wear a tunic with buttons on it, make sure there are none missing. Your clothes should be ironed if necessary.

Your appearance gives certain messages about you, so think carefully about what sort of image you intend to project. For example, if you have body piercings and tattoos some clients may find that off-putting. How formal or informal you look is up to you, but you need to look business-like and extremely clean and tidy. Ideally, you should have designated work clothes. This gives a professional impression, puts you into 'work mode', and gives some separation between your work and free time. Remember that first impressions count for a lot. Once you have made a poor impression on a client it is very difficult to change it, and you may lose that client as a result.

WORKING WITHIN A CODE OF CONDUCT

Your training school and/or professional organisation may well have given you a code of conduct, reflecting best working practice. If so, you will have an idea of what is expected of the professional therapist. Fundamentally, this should lead to the practitioner working for the highest good of their patient. A good code will therefore include most or all of the following:

TOWARDS CLIENTS:

- you should behave with integrity and professionalism
- you should work for the highest good and the best interests of those you treat
- you must respect client confidentiality
- you should not attempt to give treatment beyond your ability
- you must not claim to cure medical conditions
- you must refer a client to their doctor if you suspect serious ill health (and record that you have given this advice)
- you must not abuse their trust, or cause them undue distress or embarrassment
- you should show your clients the consideration that you yourself would expect to receive
- you should provide a clean, hygienic environment for treatment

TOWARDS COLLEAGUES:
- you should behave with consideration, fairness, professionalism and integrity
- you should not criticise them
- you should not attempt to entice other people's clients to see you

TOWARDS THE MEDICAL PROFESSION:
- remember that the doctor remains responsible for the care of his/her patient
- you must seek a doctor's consent if treating someone with a serious illness (and record that you have received it)
- if the doctor refuses consent, you must not treat the patient
- you should keep a doctor informed of the progress of his patient (in writing, unless s/he specifies otherwise)
- you should try to foster good working relationships with doctors

FOR YOUR OWN PROTECTION:
- you must be adequately insured
- you must keep comprehensive records on clients
- you should maintain the highest possible standards of practice
- you should keep up to date with advances in your therapy
- you should not make exaggerated claims for your therapy either verbally, or in advertising or literature, and specifically, you must not claim to cure
- if in doubt about treating anyone, you should seek appropriate advice.

Remember, a code of conduct is not something to pay lip service to, or to opt in and out of as and when you feel like it. It is designed to help you better manage your relationships with your clients and colleagues and to enhance both your own credibility and the credibility of your profession. If you observe your professional organisation's code at all times, and incorporate it into your practice from the start, you'll be taking a key step towards becoming a successful therapist.

Insurance

Before starting work as a therapist it is vital that you research and obtain adequate insurance cover. This is also a good time to join a professional organisation, for both your credibility and their support. Many professional organisations offer insurance to their members, and this is a good way of finding the specialist cover you need. There are four main types of cover:

- public liability
- professional indemnity
- product liability
- employer's liability.

The two which will be essential for you are public liability and professional indemnity. Whether you need the other two will depend on your work circumstances.

Public liability insurance is sometimes referred to as 'trip and slip cover'. This covers you if a client (or member of the public) falls off your couch, or trips on your stairs, and sues you for negligence. You have a legal responsibility under the Health and Safety at Work Act 1974 (and the additional regulations) to ensure that the premises you work from are safe. If you're not sure how to do this, check the Health and Safety Executive website (www.hse.gov.uk) for free guidance. This also applies to clinics and complementary health centres. The owner's public liability insurance will cover them if they are deemed to be liable but it will not cover you, so do not rely on someone else's policy to protect you – it won't!

Professional indemnity insurance is to protect you if a client sues you for injury, pain, or suffering as a result of your treatment, or for things like breach of confidentiality, or libel or slander. Check that the policy covers you wherever you work and for *all* the therapies you practise. Remember, a claim against you could happen at any time – regardless of how good a therapist you are, or think you are. A client may claim that you have injured her or caused her to become ill days, weeks, or even months after you've treated her. This is, of course, a good reason to be absolutely meticulous about your record keeping and to keep your records somewhere safe and secure – you may need to refer back to your notes long after a particular treatment. Be prepared to keep your notes for some time, too – a client is allowed by law to initiate a claim up to 3 years from the date of 'discovering' the injury or illness. In the case of, for example, an alleged breach of confidentiality, she has up to 6 years in which to bring a claim. So keep your records for as long as possible from the date of any given treatment.

Product liability insurance covers you for any injury or harm suffered by anyone as a result of a defect in products which you make or supply, whether they are those you have made yourself or made by others. If you plan to sell any products you will need this cover. Under EC law, you are held to be liable even if you did not know that the product was defective.

Employer's liability insurance cover, provided by an authorised insurer to the value of at least £5M, is an *absolute legal requirement* if you intend to employ staff. (The only exception which may possibly apply to you is if all your employees are closely related to you – e.g. sister, cousin, father, grandmother – and you are a sole trader or partnership. If your employees are all family members and you trade as a limited company, you must still take out employer's liability cover.) This cover means that you will be able to meet claims for compensation if a member of your staff has an accident on your premises and sues you for negligence. Make sure, too, that your policy covers your legal fees in case an employee tries to sue you.

Don't even think about putting off getting employer's liability cover. As well as putting yourself and your employees at risk, you will also be committing an offence, for which you can be fined up to £2,500 (for any day for which you are without appropriate insurance). In addition, if you don't display your insurance certificate, or show it to Health and Safety Executive inspectors if and when they ask to see it, you will be liable to a fine of up to £1,000.

In addition, you should consider taking out cover for your premises, known as buildings insurance. If you work from home, this will probably take the form of household and contents insurance. In this case you must inform your insurers of both your buildings and contents that you work from home. Most household policies require that the premises are used solely for domestic purposes, so you may invalidate your insurance if you don't tell them. If you own or rent premises for your work, make sure you have cover for damage to those premises – if you rent, you'll need to check whether it is you or your landlord who is responsible for obtaining cover.

Similarly, think about obtaining cover for your business equipment. If you work from home, you'll need to check whether your household/buildings insurance covers your business equipment as well – some do, some don't. If yours doesn't, ask your household insurer to quote for the extra cover you need. If they don't offer such cover, find another insurer who does – if your work equipment is stolen or gets damaged and your household insurance does not include it, you won't be able to make a claim. You may even be invalidating your existing cover, which will leave you without cover for your home.

Although not legally required for your business, buildings and contents insurance could make the difference between the survival and failure of your business if, for example, you are unfortunate enough to be on the wrong end of a break-in or a bad case of flooding. Think about everything you use for your business – for example, a computer, printer, telephone, filing cabinet, couch, oils, towels, and so on – could you afford to replace everything at once if you had to? If not, then consider getting cover against this type of possibility. The cost will only amount to a few pounds a month, which will not only ensure peace of mind but will be greatly preferable to having to pay out hundreds of pounds all in one go!

Other types of insurance you might want to think about include health insurance and business interruption insurance. Private health insurance is virtually a must if you are self employed, since your income is entirely dependent on you being fit and well. In addition, consider taking out income replacement insurance. For example, if you broke your arm and couldn't work, having income replacement insurance will mean that you will receive a proportion of your usual income for the period you are out of action. Be careful to check the exclusions and excesses, though, before taking out a policy, particularly if you have had particular illnesses or injuries in the past. It is also possible to obtain cover for the cost of employing a locum.

Business interruption insurance cover does what the name suggests – it helps you to continue your business if something happens that would otherwise prevent you from doing so, such as your premises being badly damaged. Some may cover you for the shortfall in your usual profits, others will pay out for a temporary workspace and any professional fees you incur in the meantime. Exactly what the policy covers and compensates you for depends very much on each insurer, so again, make sure you read all the small print thoroughly before signing up for cover.

If you use your car for your practice, check the terms of your car insurance to see whether your work equipment is covered. If not, think about taking out additional cover. If you spend most of your working week out and about, car theft poses a real risk. But have a look first at your household contents insurance – it may already cover your car contents (though again, not if those contents are used specifically for your business).

Given all the different types of insurance cover available, and all the various exclusions and excesses, it makes sense to discuss your insurance needs in detail with a specialist (who may be a broker) – there are several listed at the end of the book. A good specialist will be able to advise you and help you make the right choices to match your specific requirements, and won't try to sell you cover that is superfluous to your needs. Whatever you do – get several quotes, and always read and check the small print carefully before handing over your money!

Methods of payment

The most common methods of payment to individual practitioners are cheques and cash. You can also arrange to accept payment by BACS (direct bank transfer), debit card or credit card. If you accept credit cards you will have to pay a fee per transaction and with both credit and debit cards, you will have to purchase the equipment to process payments.

Boundaries

Most complementary therapies involve touch. The need for safe, non-sexual, caring human touch is universal: it is that very need which often brings people to complementary therapies. Yet society is ambivalent about touch. We have become so politically correct that teachers refrain from cuddling children who are upset and sports coaches avoid touching athletes for fear of damaging their reputation. As a society we seem to be teaching our children to be afraid of touch, rather than to be confident in differentiating between appropriate and inappropriate touch.

The touch we employ in practising our therapies, though appropriate, can be more personal and intimate than some people are used to. Even getting undressed can be an ordeal and we need to be aware that being almost naked on a treatment couch makes our clients vulnerable.

It may be that a client does not realise what your treatment involves. It may be that something has happened to them in the past which affects their ability to trust you. It is part of your job to find a way of treating them that does not reactivate their distress.

In order to avoid misunderstandings and minimise any anxiety, it is essential that you are clear about your own boundaries and those of your client. Your clients will bring their own 'baggage' to your session. It is vital that they trust you and that you do not betray that trust in any way. If your clients have to undress for a treatment, and you have skin-to-skin contact with them, you need to be especially aware of the potential for misunderstanding.

Remember that clients may not immediately admit to traumas in their past. It is common for them to take some time to trust you enough to divulge such things. For this reason you could be 'treading on their corns' without the slightest intention of distressing them. As I have said before, clients may not tell you that they are unhappy with what you have done, they just won't come back.

We ourselves are also vulnerable, because we are viewed as caring, compassionate people, and that care can be open to misinterpretation. Good communication is the key to a happy professional relationship. You should explain what is involved in your treatment as fully as you can and say that if there is anything the client is unhappy about, you will stop at once. The client needs to feel in control, not as if they have to lie back and endure what you choose for them. If you need to work near an area that might be contentious, such as the breasts, explain why you need to do this and ask your client's permission. I always do, even with clients I have treated over many years. Should your client refuse, you must respect their decision (and with good grace) even if you feel less able to give a good treatment.

You also convey trust by the intention of your touch. Anyone who has been in a crowded place knows the difference between a 'grope' and accidental contact. If the intention behind your touch is always professional your client is more likely to feel comfortable with you. Once trust is established any accidental touch is more easily explained as an accident. Equally, once you have lost a client's trust, you are likely to have lost the client.

There is a charitable organisation called WITNESS that trains professionals in establishing and maintaining healthy boundaries. It also supports people who have been assaulted by health care workers. There is more information on their website www.professionalboundaries.org.uk

'SPECIAL TREATMENTS' LICENCES

Because of local authority legislation, many beauty cosmetic and complementary treatments and therapies now have to be licensed. There are 2 types of special treatment licence:

- one for 'establishments' in which special treatments are carried out, and
- another for therapists and others working in premises which offer special treatments. These individuals must themselves be registered to provide the treatment(s).

If you advertise or give a 'special treatment' and don't have a licence, you could be liable to a fine of up to £2,500.

IF YOU'RE AN INDIVIDUAL THERAPIST . . .

Let's say that you give reflexology treatments one day a week in a local complementary therapy clinic. The clinic itself will almost certainly need a licence. If it has a licence, then – unless you are exempted – you will need an individual licence in order to work there.

There are some exemptions to licences for individuals – these depend on your particular therapy, qualifications, membership body, and insurance cover. Each local authority differs slightly with regard to exemptions (and some still don't require any licence at all), so contact yours to make absolutely sure whether you need to be licensed or not.

The good news is that most authorities don't charge for individual licences, most licences last for 3 years or more, and applying is very straightforward. Be aware, though, that you will need an individual licence for every different local authority area that you work in – something to watch out for if you travel around a bit.

For example, if you are based in Wandsworth, but work in clinics in Barnet and Islington as well, then you potentially need 3 licences (depending on whether you qualify for exemption) – one for each local authority area you work in.

If you run premises providing 'special treatments' . . .

An establishment that requires a 'special treatment' licence is any premises intended for the use of all sorts of therapies and treatments – for example, massage, manicures, acupuncture, chiropody, osteopathy, reflexology, and so on.

You'll probably fall under this category if you run a complementary therapy clinic, a set of therapy rooms, a spa, a beauty salon, or even a hairdressing salon which offers a few therapies as a sideline.

Unlike the licences for individual therapists, licences for premises are usually subject to a fee. These can vary hugely, from no fee at all to several hundred pounds, depending on your local authority, how many therapists you have, and how many treatments your premises offers.

Contact your local authority's licensing department for details. They'll be able to provide you with an application pack and will be able to tell you how much a licence costs.

IF YOUR LOCAL AUTHORITY DOESN'T LICENSE 'SPECIAL TREATMENTS' YET . . .

. . . make sure you check with them every so often so that you don't get caught out. Any councils that don't yet license special treatments will almost certainly eventually do so – and many are currently reviewing their licensing arrangements or are due to do so imminently.

Be alert!

CHECKLIST

- ❏ have you put in place all your tax and insurance needs? (more on this in Chapters 9 and 11)
- ❏ are you conversant with your code of conduct, and do you understand why it is so important?
- ❏ is your hygiene and appearance of a professional standard?
- ❏ have you decided what you will wear for work?
- ❏ do you practise integrity in your life?
- ❏ have you thought about what might put potential clients off?
- ❏ is all your paperwork, such as consent forms and case history sheets, in order?
- ❏ are you clear about your own professional boundaries and how that impacts on your clients?
- ❏ have you checked with your local authority as to whether you need a special licence?

2 SETTING UP YOUR PRACTICE

Work is love made visible   KAHLIL GIBRAN, *THE PROPHET*

What sort of practice do you envisage? Will you work
- from home?
- in a complementary therapy clinic?
- by providing home visits or on-site massage?
- at a GP's surgery?
- at a physiotherapy/osteopathic/chiropractic clinic?
- at a leisure centre?
- at a health farm?
- at a hairdresser's or beauty therapist's?
- at a combination of the above?

What will you offer?
- a clinical environment
- a homely atmosphere
- incense and new age music
- your front room, with the children watching TV and the dog barking

What kind of people do you want to treat? For the most part you will need clients who are solvent with a reasonable disposable income, some of which they are prepared to spend with you. You, too, need to pay your bills and eat, so it is essential to think about where your clients will come from and what you want them to pay you.

Much will depend on your background and past career(s). In order to be successful you will need to find your niche in the market. Ask yourself why people would prefer to see you than therapist B down the road. What makes your treatment special? Are you good at de-stressing people? Are you good at remedial work? Are you a good listener?

I have a nursing background. I receive a lot of referrals from physiotherapists, doctors and osteopaths. I have a basic knowledge of how the body works (and what happens when it doesn't!) and I know my limitations in practice. I treat lots of bad backs, arthritis and the like. I also lecture to nurses and therapists on massage and complementary therapies and business skills.

A colleague (who isn't a nurse) is just as busy as me, concentrating on de-stressing businessmen. If someone calls her asking her to mobilise a healed fracture, she suggests they call me instead. We are both established in massage. We are successful because we have thought about what we are good at and have worked to develop that as an area of practice.

This is extremely important. There are many people training in complementary therapies and standards vary enormously. You will need to sell not only your therapy, but your ability as a therapist and your personality as well. It may take time to develop confidence in yourself as a therapist, but if you are competent, professional in your attitude, and welcoming, people will come to see you. If you make them feel that you really value and care about them they will be loyal clients for many years to come.

■ ARRANGING YOUR WORK TO SUIT YOU

WORKING HOURS

Planning the hours you will work may not seem terribly relevant when you only see a couple of clients per week. However, you expect your practice to grow busier, and it is important that it grows in a way you want, and that it doesn't take you unaware. It is frustrating to find you have one client every day, when if they came one after another you could use your free time more fruitfully. It is important to treat people when it is convenient for both you and the client, so that you are not constantly at their beck and call because you need the money! If you do that you will become exhausted and less efficient as well.

You need to consider the following:

- how many hours/days per week do you plan to work?
- how many treatments will you do per day?
- will you offer evenings and weekends?
- if so, how many and how late?
- do you need to fit part time therapy with another job?
- if so, how does this impact on your working hours?
- what proportion of your income do you want to come from therapy?
- how will your working hours impact on your energy levels?

WHERE TO WORK

It is perfectly possible to earn your living working in a variety of places. If you wanted you could do, for example, one day a week in a clinic, a day at a health spa, two days at home and a day of home visits. Such variety can be good, because you have all the advantages of each work place without getting too bogged down with the disadvantages. You can choose what works best for you. The following reflects the choices available.

COMPLEMENTARY THERAPY CLINICS

There are now clinics in most cities, towns and villages in the UK. Some charge a sessional rate plus a deposit, while others ask for a percentage of your takings. The percentage rate can work to your advantage when you are starting out and may not have many clients.

Points to consider about a clinic:

- will you get on well with the owner?
- will you be allowed to work in the way you would choose?
- how many other therapists are there in your discipline?
- who are the other therapists, and what are they like?
- where is the clinic situated?
- are there adequate parking facilities for you and your clients (and does it matter if there are not?)
- is the equipment provided, such as a couch, suitable for you?
- what other support will be provided? Will there be receptionists, telephone, fax, photocopying, washing facilities, towels, couch covers and paper couch rolls?
- will the clinic provide any clients, or do you have you find them all yourself?
- are there likely to be any additional costs, such as advertising?
- how does the clinic ensure that new clients are allocated fairly to therapists?
- who 'owns' clients in the event that you move on from the clinic?
- how much notice do you have to give when leaving?

- what flexibility is there over the hours your room is available?
- under what circumstances would you lose your deposit?

Working in a clinic which is a local centre of excellence can be a great start for the fledgling therapist. The clinic will already be attracting the right clientele and you will gain a lot from the stimulation of being with other, more experienced therapists. There are likely to be people around when you need advice. You do not lose privacy as you would when working at home, and most equipment will be provided for you.

This sounds ideal and it can be. But let's look further. Are you sure that this really is a thriving clinic, or is it just a building where 30 therapists come for half a day each and fight for what little work there is? Assure yourself that the person who uses the room before you leaves it in a habitable state. Look carefully at the owner. I once worked in a clinic where the owner insisted on seeing all new clients herself for a first consultation. The theory was that she would then refer to other therapists as appropriate. In fact, she continued to treat them all herself, while telling us that we were not making enough effort to attract clients!

In another clinic, the owner insisted that all therapists trained in an additional discipline as she wanted all clients treated in a particular way. She charged the therapists a lot of money for her training and they had very little say in the way they could work.

Having said all that, I have kept in touch with many of the therapists that I met while working in clinics. They were all extremely good at their job, and I have learned a great deal from them.

The advantages of working in a clinic are:
- it is a suitable environment and equipment is provided
- you have a ready-made address and phone number
- cleaning and heating are provided
- photocopying and fax facilities are usually available
- it may be a ready-made source of clients
- you may gain support and stimulation from other therapists
- it is likely to be advertised locally and should attract appropriate clientele
- no loss of privacy, no wear and tear on your home

The disadvantages of working in a clinic are:
- it will involve some financial outlay, regardless of income
- there may be competition from other therapists
- the owner may expect you to fit in with their views on treatment
- rent increases are usually beyond your control
- the owner may try to take the larger share of clients
- clients may not be allocated fairly among therapists – receptionists can be biased!

Ask the clinic to give you an agreement in writing. An agreement is important so that both parties know what is expected of them, and to make sure no misunderstandings arise. If a clinic won't give you anything in writing, you should question their professionalism and ask yourself whether you really want to work with them. Any genuinely professional and 'above board' outfit won't have a problem with putting things in writing.

If the clinic gives you an agreement to sign, read it carefully to make sure you understand what your rights and obligations are. Does it say clearly how much you'll be paid, when, and how (e.g. cash, cheque, or BACS)? Does it state what equipment you'll be provided with? Does it allow you to mention the clinic in your promotional literature or on your website? How much notice will you get of rent increases? These are all matters which a thorough agreement will deal with.

If there's anything you don't like the look of, be prepared to negotiate – there's no point in agreeing to something that you don't feel comfortable with or are unsure about. Suggest the changes you'd like to make to the agreement. Again, a good clinic will do its best to address your concerns and aim to deal with them in a way that is acceptable to you both.

RENTING AN OFFICE

You may like to consider renting an office, if it is suitable for your therapy. There are now places you can rent on a sessional basis.

Advantages of renting sessional office space:
- it costs less than paying for full-time use
- a receptionist, a waiting area, office equipment and cleaning are provided
- it presents you in a business-like way
- it may provide parking for your clients.

Disadvantages of renting office space:
- it may not be available out of normal office hours
- it may not be a suitable environment for your therapy
- you may not be able to store your equipment there

- there may be no other therapists there
- it may not provide the sort of atmosphere you want
- you may pay a substantial premium for the services laid on for you, depending on their quality and extent. Make sure you don't end up paying for facilities you and your clients won't ever use. Check the rental agreement carefully.

WORKING AT HOME

Many therapists choose to work at home. This is often the simplest option when starting out as it involves the least financial commitment. Working at home may seem ideal, but it is actually a mixed blessing. There is no extra outlay for rent, but loss of privacy is a big disadvantage. You may feel that this is not a problem when you only see a couple of people a week. But once your practice grows it becomes more of an issue, especially when you could have 20 or so people tramping through your home.

Points to consider about working from home:
- do you have a suitable room to use for treatment?
- do you have a ground floor room?
- are you able to provide access for the disabled?
- do you need planning consent or a licence from your local council?
- can you provide a quiet environment?
- can you heat just that room or will it have to be your entire home?
- are you able to keep your working space clean and tidy?
- are you able to keep the outside of your home clean and tidy?

- how will you cope with the additional laundry?
- do you have parking facilities? (and does it matter if not?)
- do you mind having strangers in your home?
- do you mind people making personal comments on your home, decor and/or garden?

It is difficult to exercise control over who comes to your home, particularly if you advertise. Spend time talking to people when they phone – not only does it make you appear friendly and interested, it is a vital opportunity to sift out anyone undesirable. Should you end up with anyone you would rather not see again, you can be left feeling rather vulnerable because they know where you live. However, it has been my experience that unsuitable clients have not returned to cause problems. This has been true of telephone calls, too.

Whether or not you choose to work from home depends on the suitability of your living accommodation, whether you can provide parking, and how quiet the environment is.

Keep all doors shut except your treatment room – no one will be impressed by the sight of your unmade bed! You may like to have some signs such as 'Private' or 'Toilet' on your doors. You are now obliged by law to display a 'No smoking' sign. This gives the correct impression and minimises the opportunity for misunderstanding. You could leave a few children's toys around if you want to give the impression of having a family.

The areas to which your clients have access need to be spotless and tidy. This can be difficult for those with small children. Avoid leaving washing on the radiators, as it looks unsightly and unprofessional. Your treatment room and bathroom must be spotless. Your clients will not be impressed if your 5-year-old didn't flush the toilet. If you have to share your bathroom with clients leave as few clues to your personal life as possible. Equally, the entrance to your premises and its driveway and garden also need to be tidy. Plant tubs and hanging baskets should be well cared for. Your windows should be clean, and as I write this, I see that my front door needs painting!

One disadvantage of working at home crops up if you have noisy family, neighbours or friends. A psychotherapist friend tells of seeing a new client for the first time on the day her 18-year-old left school. The girl had celebrated in the pub with her friends and returned home incapable of coordinating key and lock. She rang the doorbell endlessly, while the poor psychotherapist tried to concentrate on her client. As she ushered him out, her drunken daughter fell through the door and vomited on the floor. The client was still within earshot as my friend yelled furiously at her daughter. (The client continued to see her for four years, so it wasn't a total disaster.)

It is worth mentioning that not all clients like New Age music and incense. Do bear in mind that some people really treasure silence or dislike certain kinds of music and their preference should be respected. I remember having a beauty treatment in a salon. The therapist left me for a while with loud pop music playing. I would have loved peace and quiet, or some classical or New Age music, but was instead forced to listen to something I didn't like. I never went back there.

Another possible disadvantage of working from home is that you will need to buy and store all your own equipment such as a couch and towels. I would suggest that you buy as good quality a couch as possible. There is more on choosing equipment in Chapter 3.

If your therapy involves the use of items such as towels and couch covers, you will need to consider whether you can manage the extra laundry. My washing machine takes enough towels for two clients at a time. If you do six treatments a day your washing machine will have to take three loads of towels before you have done any personal laundry. Laundry services are worth looking into: there are some which provide the towels as well as washing them. They can also help if your washing machine lets you down. My local dry cleaner does a service wash which I use in a crisis. It is wise to research your back-up plan before you need it.

The advantages of working at home:
- the work environment is likely to be within your control
- you have complete autonomy over the way you work
- there is no financial outlay for rent/deposit
- it is easier to absorb fluctuations in income
- if you have young children, you may be still able to work if they are unwell
- your clients may prefer it.

The disadvantages of working at home:
- you may feel isolated
- you may appear less professional than working away from home
- your home environment has to be consistently well maintained and tidy
- there may be no one around if you are treating a client you're unhappy with
- you have to buy all the necessary equipment e.g. couch/telephone/filing cabinet

- you have to bear the cost of heating, lighting and laundry
- you bear the cost of advertising
- the onus is on you to find clients
- you will sacrifice some privacy
- noises of neighbours, children, doorbells, telephone, TV, etc., may cause distraction
- clients may phone at inconvenient times because they know you are there.

If, after considering all your options, working at home seems like an attractive option, check your title deeds and mortgage terms if you own your own house or flat. Is there anything in the deeds, such as a covenant, which prohibits you from running a business in your home? If so, ask your solicitor to see what can be done. Breaching a covenant could land you in court. Similarly, is there anything in your lender's mortgage terms about whether you can run a business at home? Be very careful – by breaching a mortgage term, you could invalidate your mortgage.

If you rent your home, check your lease to see if there is a prohibition on business activities. If there is, don't ignore it – you could give your landlord a reason to give you notice. Very occasionally, there are local by-laws preventing people from running businesses from their homes – so check with your local authority to see whether there are any such by-laws affecting you.

You should also contact your local council to find out whether – if you are a home owner – you need consent for 'change of use'. It is usually only necessary to obtain consent if your home (or more than half of it) is to be used exclusively for your business. (If it will be used exclusively for business, bear in mind also that you may become liable to pay business rates to your local authority.) If you use your treatment room for work for eight hours a day and for the remaining 16 hours it doubles up as a library/study/spare bedroom, you should not need consent. It would be sensible to ask your local council for written confirmation that this is the case.

And, of course, if you're contemplating knocking down walls, or doing any other structural work in connection with making your home business-worthy, remember to check with the council about the possible need for planning permission and Building Regulations consent.

Finally, working at home doesn't exempt you from Health and Safety rules and regulations. Whether you own or rent, if you are 'in control' of work premises, then you must be comply with The Health and Safety at Work Act 1974, which is concerned with protecting the health and safety of everyone who uses your premises. It's a serious issue: it is actually illegal to run your business unless you comply with the Act and the additional regulations. The cost of ignoring the law? In 2006/7, the average fine for non-compliance was £15,370.

The good news is that if you work on your own at home, then you should be able to comply with Health and Safety requirements without having to get someone to help you. The basics of complying couldn't be easier. It's mostly a matter of using commonsense and trying to make sure that no one is at risk from getting ill or injured on your premises.

What you need to do is
- carry out a risk assessment
- deal with any risks that you identify

- make sure you have a procedure in place for continuing to check the risks from time to time.

The key is to decide whether a hazard (which could be anything from electricity cables, essential oil burners, or acupuncture needles through to steep steps or slippery flooring), presents a real risk, and whether that risk has been made as small as possible.

Let's say, for example, that there is a small step down into your treatment room from your hallway. You may be well used to it, but it is almost certainly a risk that someone who is unfamiliar with your house would miss it, and potentially stumble and fall. It is therefore a potential hazard. Now you must deal with it appropriately to get rid of the risk altogether or to minimise it as far as you can. You can do this in a number of possible ways. For example, you could:

- mark the edges with brightly-coloured tape
- put up a poster over or by the door – visible to everyone – to point out the step and to warn others to take care when entering the room.

You don't need to write down your assessment findings, although it's a good idea, because:

- you'll have a record for your own reference – so that you know what to check next time, and what to keep an eye on
- it'll be useful if a Health and Safety inspector comes to your premises and does a spot check, so that you can show what you've done

- if anybody ever sues you for injury or illness caused by your premises, it may prove helpful to your defence
- you'll be able to show that you've complied with the law.

Hopefully, by putting in place sensible precautionary measures, you'll never have to deal with anyone injuring themselves or falling ill in your home. But if you do find yourself in this position, under the Reporting of Injuries, Diseases and Dangerous Occurrences Regulations 1995 (RIDDOR), you must also be diligent about reporting any such accidents or illnesses that first occur on your premises. All the details of how to do this are on the RIDDOR website at www.riddor.gov.uk

Whatever you do, be sure to get as much help and advice as possible from the Health and Safety Executive (their website, www.hse.gov.uk, is very useful and clear) and your local council to make absolutely sure that you comply with all the relevant regulations.

HOME VISITS

Home visits are worth considering if your home is not suitable and you do not wish to work in a clinic. There are advantages for the therapist but also disadvantages in not being able to control what happens there. The biggest advantage is for the client, who will be able to relax afterwards instead of battling through traffic to get home.

Remember to take into account the time you will spend travelling and the wear and tear on your car (and on you, carting your couch around). There may be nowhere to park your car. It may be that the room you do the treatment in is up lots of flights of stairs. It could be barely big enough to get your couch into, making it difficult to work properly. You won't know any of this until you have been somewhere for the first time. You will also need to be extra vigilant in someone else's home. A colleague tells of the time she went to do some waxing. The client's young son burst into the room and knocked over the pot of hot wax onto the new, immaculate (until then) white carpet. I once caught an antique vase with my bag and knocked it onto the floor. Fortunately it didn't break. On another occasion I had to treat a client with a large Labrador sitting on my feet. It refused to move until I had given it some massage.

Points to consider about home visits are:
- do you need a car to transport your equipment? If so, check the terms of your insurance policy – you may need to change it in order to cover your business use
- is your 'portable' couch truly portable?
- do you have an answering machine/mobile phone?
- how much will you charge for the extra time you spend travelling?
- you will need to allow extra time for setting up
- how large an area are you prepared to cover?
- are you good at map reading, or do you have satellite navigation?
- can you work comfortably on someone else's 'home ground'?
- are you good at finding a suitable spot to work in someone else's house?
- are you good at keeping to schedule?
- are you easily waylaid by offers of cups of tea or clients who are not ready when you arrive?

- are you able to adapt what you do to fit the client's environment?
- do you mind clients with animals?
- are you able to concentrate in less than ideal circumstances?

I went to treat a man, his wife and their daughter at their house as the man was seriously ill. His wife asked me to treat him in bed. There was a large wooden frame round the outside of the bed, making it impossible to get near enough to treat him comfortably. When I dragged my aching back downstairs, I was asked to set up my couch in their sitting room. The phone rang constantly (8 times in the first hour.) The grandchildren insisted on playing under the couch, and 'Bob the Builder' was blaring from the TV. Each time I asked the children to lower the volume they did, but then put it up again when they thought I wouldn't notice. An electrician was drilling through the wall in the loft. The cleaner, gardener, and electrician walked past my semi-naked client and me several times. A neighbour popped in, talking at length to my client on the couch and kept touching her while I waited to continue working. Eventually I left and came face to face with another car coming up the drive. I reversed to allow him in, damaging my car on a low wall in the process. He did not even thank me.

This is no exaggeration. When you visit someone in their own home you have absolutely no control over what happens there. I left these clients feeling stressed because I didn't think I had given them my usual standard of treatments. Eventually the man died and I was able to ask the other members of the family to come to me once more.

Not all home visits are as difficult as that. The advantages of home visits are:

- there is no loss of privacy for you
- no one will know whether your home is tidy or not
- there is no wear and tear on your furniture and carpets
- there is no substantial financial outlay, assuming you already have a car
- the client bears the cost of heating and lighting
- the client can relax afterwards instead of having to get themselves home.

The disadvantages of home visits are:

- they may not provide an ideal work environment and you may not be able to do anything about that
- you may not be easy to contact if you are away from home for long periods
- there will be wear and tear on your car
- it is more difficult to impose your time schedule in someone else's home
- a larger proportion of your day will be spent travelling rather than practising your therapy
- you are at greater risk of threats to your personal safety
- you must take great care to avoid spills or breakages.

CORPORATE CLIENTS

Some therapists like to work within corporate organisations. It can be difficult to convince companies of the benefits your skills will bring them, so it may be easier to work for an organisation that sends therapists into the workplace. If you are successful in finding a company that will allow you to treat their staff in the workplace,

you will need to decide the following:
- is there a suitable room you can use for the treatments?
- how frequently will you go there?
- how will you protect client confidentiality?
- how will you ensure good hygiene in this workplace?
- is there somewhere the client can rest after a treatment?
- will the client be able to rest after a treatment?
- what are the arrangements for payment – does the client pay all, part or none of your fee?

Advantages of corporate work:
- the clients are already there for you
- you may be able to spend a substantial amount of time in one place
- the employer may subsidise treatments
- clients do not have to travel to see you
- you will not bear any cost of heating or lighting
- you may gain clients you would not otherwise have reached with your advertising or marketing.

Disadvantages of corporate work:
- clients may prefer to have treatments away from their work environment
- if they have to return to work immediately it may reduce the benefit of your treatment
- you may have to take a couch, towels, oils and equipment with you each time you visit
- they may prefer that their work colleagues do not know that they have treatments (particularly if you are a counsellor)

- they may have to cancel their session at short notice or
  fail to attend because they are unable to leave work
- if the company pays you, you may not be
  paid immediately

If you find corporate work on your own account (instead of through an organisation which places therapists with corporate clients), try to get an agreement in writing with the company. For one thing, it makes you look more professional and enhances your credibility. Companies sign agreements all the time, so they are unlikely to be put out if you ask for one. If they suggest that you provide them with an agreement, try to get one drafted professionally. That way, you can be reasonably sure that it covers all the bases.

What many companies don't have much experience of is having therapists coming into their workplace and, for that reason, they don't necessarily appreciate what facilities and support you might need to ensure that you – and they – are happy with the arrangement. So, if you write an agreement for them to sign, here are some examples of the kinds of requirements you might have:

- that they allocate someone specific who is your point
  of contact at all times, and who has a deputy if
  necessary. You don't want to turn up only to find that
  your 'contact' is off sick, and that nobody knows who
  you are or why you're there!
- that a quiet room is made available, with whatever
  facilities you need, such as a couple of chairs, a small
  table, a water dispenser, and so on
- that the company 'contact' is responsible for

advertising your services in the company, takes bookings, and lets you know how many clients (and their names) you can expect to see

- that you have the right to cancel a scheduled visit to the company if insufficient clients are booked to see you
- that the company pays you, by whatever method you prefer, within 30 days (or sooner, if you prefer) of the date of your invoice. Don't be shy of asking for prompt payment – company payment procedures can be a bit slow, so it's worth letting them know as clearly as possible what your payment terms are.

As with any agreement, but particularly if the company produces its own for you to sign, negotiate over any points you're not comfortable with, and be prepared to walk away if you don't feel comfortable with anything. You don't have to work there!

BUYING A PRACTICE

Buying a practice is not usually the first priority of a newly qualified therapist. But you might have a big vision and want to do it your way right from the start, and/or you might have therapist friends and colleagues with whom you want to go into business and with whom you can share the financial risk.

Occasionally, too, the opportunity may arise for you to buy an existing practice with ready-made clients. Your local paper is a good place to look. If having your own practice appeals to you, then this is likely to be a highly attractive option.

Buying a practice is a considerable undertaking. You will almost certainly take on a commercial lease, buy business assets and goodwill, and take on staff, whether as employees or as freelance contractors, or both. It's important that you get things right, or you could find yourself struggling before you even open for business. Don't take unnecessary risks – get professional advice and engage a commercial solicitor and a good accountant to look after the purchase and all the related legal and financial issues.

Spas

Spas are often looking for therapists, and if you like the idea it is worth contacting those near you. You will be working in an appropriate environment, usually with good support, and they may provide you with further training. As elsewhere, try to make sure you get something in writing, and check the agreement for possible problem issues before you sign.

However, you might be expected to work to a timetable that is geared to treating as many clients per day as possible. This could be exhausting. You would probably earn more per treatment working elsewhere, but you will gain lots of experience which is useful when you are setting out. It also looks good on your CV or brochure to say that you have worked there. A disadvantage is that you will not build a client base long term, though regular visitors may request you. However, you will certainly grow in confidence as you deal with such variety.

Travel and holiday resorts

Cruise liners, airlines and hotels in holiday resorts may offer excellent opportunities for travel, but possibly little opportunity to see the countries you visit. Again, the working environment is likely to be good (unless you are squashed into a corner of an airport terminal building) with clients, equipment and uniform provided.

The NHS

There are so many changes within the NHS that it is difficult to provide up-to-date information on it. Normally, if a GP practice wants you to treat their patients, you are given an NHS provider number, which you must quote on your invoices, and you will be paid by the local Primary Care Trust. Be warned that this can sometimes take quite a few weeks, and you may have to chase up payment.

Osteopaths/chiropractors/ physiotherapists

They may have a room you could rent on a sessional basis and, being in complementary practice themselves, are more likely to identify patients you could help. You would need to be interested in and knowledgeable about bodywork and be able to work with other health professionals. They also might expect you to have some experience and would probably appreciate seeing your certificates and CV.

Hospices/homes for the elderly/hospitals

The way to get in to these areas is often to offer to work voluntarily, but it is possible that you could be paid. Some therapists have begun as volunteers and have progressed to being paid at a later date.

Do not be downcast if your offers are rejected. Keep offering your services and you will find your niche. It is important to know what you want and aim for that. Don't waste time chasing job opportunities which you know are not suitable for you.

Working with vulnerable adults and/or children

If you plan to work with vulnerable people, you may be asked to undertake a Criminal Records Bureau (CRB) check. This can take some time, so it is as well to apply in good time. An enhanced check is typically required if you plan to work with vulnerable adults. This means that a CRB check is done first, then a further check is done by one or more police forces. There is more information on www.crb.gov.uk

Be aware, too, that there may be an issue over whether your clients, as vulnerable adults or children, can give valid consent to treatment or whether someone else has authority (e.g. by power of attorney) to give consent on their behalf. If you are unsure, ask whoever cares for them – for example, the local authority, a relative, or private care home – about this before you carry out any treatment.

Working with vulnerable people: the law and new developments from 2009

At the moment, it's not a legal requirement for you if you are a self-employed therapist to have a Criminal Records Bureau (CRB) check, although employers may ask you to have one. However, there will be major changes when new legislation (principally, the Safeguarding Vulnerable Groups Act 2006) comes into effect in October 2009.

The Independent Safeguarding Authority (ISA) has been created to help prevent unsuitable people from working with children and vulnerable adults. The ISA will work in partnership with the Criminal Records Bureau, and will assess each individual who wants to work or volunteer to work with vulnerable people, whether they are self employed or employees. The most important point to note with this new change is that once the new Act comes into force, it will be an offence (if you work with vulnerable people and those under the age of 18) not to register with the ISA. The penalties for not registering are a fine or up to five years in prison.

Potential employees and volunteers will need to apply to register with the ISA. Self employed people can apply through the ISA website while the vetting service is being phased in. There will be a one off registration fee, and you will be given a personal ISA registration number which is unique to you. You will therefore remain on the ISA database even if you are an employee and change employers.

For the definition of 'vulnerable' under the Act, and for more information on the ISA more generally, visit the ISA website, at www.isa-gov.org.uk

CHECKLIST

- ❏ have you decided on the kind of practice you want?
- ❏ have you thought about your niche in the market ?
- ❏ have you planned your hours and place/s of work?
- ❏ do you comply with Health and Safety regulations?
- ❏ do you need a Criminal Records Bureau check?

3 CHOOSING AND BUYING EQUIPMENT

Take your profession seriously. Don't take yourself seriously.

CLINT EASTWOOD

SETTING YOUR BUDGET

It is important to set a realistic budget for your new business and keep to it as closely as possible. Cheapest is not necessarily best, and good quality equipment will help to create a professional business-like image. Not only that, the most suitable equipment will enable you to work effectively and conserve your energy. Fortunately, the costs of setting up your business are relatively small unless you intend to buy a practice straightaway. Depending on your therapy and whether you work from home or not, you will probably need to buy a couch, covers and towels, oils, a business phone, stationery, and set up a website and do some advertising. The cost of this can mount up, so it makes sense to decide what is vital and what might wait for a while.

ADVERTISING

Advertising, in particular, is a bottomless pit into which you could easily sink all your money. One disadvantage of advertising in phone books such as Yellow Pages and Thomson's Directory is that other advertisers use them to call you and ask you to advertise with them as well. This can be irritating if you consider you have already spent your budget, but remember you can always say no. Advertising companies do not always understand that what might be a small outlay for a larger business is a huge amount for a one-man band. I used to advertise in the main directories. They didn't actually bring me much work directly, but my existing clients would pass on my name, telling others that they could find my phone number in the directories.

In fact, your best advertising is likely to be free – your clients will quickly spread the word if they are happy with your treatments. It may be a slower way to grow your business, but it is by far the most effective. In my practice, one or two particularly satisfied people have recommended a lot of new clients to me.

Phone

Many therapists now use a mobile phone as their main business point of contact. If you decide to do this, it is worth investigating the business schemes that mobile phone providers offer. Normally the best deals are with contracts rather than pay as you go.

The advantages of mobile phones are:
- you can make calls when away from home
- you can access calls when away from home
- you can contact some of your clients, and they you, by text message
- others are less likely to answer your mobile phone
- you can keep it as a dedicated business phone

The disadvantages of a mobile phone are:
- it can be difficult to separate work and personal life unless you have two phone numbers
- your clients may call you at inconvenient times because they know you will answer
- you may not appear professional if you answer business calls when socialising

- you need to remember to keep it charged all the time
- you may not be able to make appointments if your clients call at an inconvenient time
- you may find yourself in areas with no signal.

If you choose to use a landline for business, it may be possible to have two different numbers with different ring tones on the same phone so you can differentiate between work and personal calls. This is helpful if someone else might answer the phone. It can detract from your professional image if others answer your business phone and also if they fail to pass on messages. If a lot of people use your landline, it may be better to install a second line which is dedicated to your business. This also saves you the tedious chore of working out which calls are personal and which are business when submitting the bill to your accountant. You could also consider having a free phone number to induce potential clients to call you.

Your landline phone will need an answering service of some kind; there are some that allow you to access messages when away from home if you need to do so. If you plan to site the phone in the room you will be working in, it is useful to choose a phone with a ringer that you can turn off. This ensures that you and your client are not disturbed during a treatment.

Advantages of a business landline are:
- you can have a dedicated business line or ring tone
- you can leave a business message on the voicemail
- if the line is out of order you can have calls transferred to your mobile
- you can have an outgoing message specially for your business

- you can ensure that you take calls when convenient to you.

Disadvantages of a business landline are:
- you may appear less professional if others answer the phone
- the ring may disturb you when you are working
- when away from home you may be out of contact with clients.

HEADED NOTEPAPER, COMPLIMENT SLIPS, AND TREATMENT VOUCHERS

In order to appear professional in your dealings, you will need to have headed notepaper, compliment slips, and vouchers if you plan to use them. You may like all your personalised literature to match, but this is not essential. Your stationery should be good quality, reflecting the fact that you are offering a quality service. Your personalised literature must give the impression that you are a professional person, providing a professional service, as this will give your potential clients the confidence that you are competent. Avoid using labels on previously used envelopes when sending letters in your professional capacity, as it may not create the right impression. You could buy good quality recycled stationery instead.

If you have a computer, you may be able to reduce the amount of printed paper you need to buy by setting up a template. This is useful for writing letters and producing bills and receipts.

BROCHURES

The first point to consider is what you intend to use your brochures for. Possibilities include:

- mass marketing – such as putting them through local letter boxes
- targeted marketing – placing in a variety of appropriate outlets
- personal marketing – handing them out personally.

Before you begin designing and writing your brochure, it is essential to emphasise correct spelling. What you practise in your practice is complementary therapy. You will have much greater credibility if you can spell what you do! I would also wonder if a person were being truthful about their achievements if they could not spell correctly or their grammar was poor. For example, I once saw a brochure stating that the therapist was a member of the 'Royal College of Nurses.' As a nurse myself, I know that should be 'Royal College of Nurs*ing*'. This led me to wonder if they were a member after all. It may be that whoever printed your brochure has made the error, but it is your credibility that is at stake, so check very carefully before agreeing to a print run.

Your brochure or leaflet is your opportunity to tell the world about your therapy and yourself. It should persuade anyone reading it that they should come to see you. It should be a true reflection of you and your practice (or what you intend your practice to be). It seems to me, therefore, that it is essential to include some information about yourself in your brochure.

Your brochure should be written with potential clients in mind. What would they want to know which would persuade them to come and see you? As your practice develops you may need more than one version of your brochure so that it is specific to the people you are targeting. Broadly, I would suggest that brochures should contain some information on:

- your therapy – what it is, its benefits and who might benefit from it
- the therapist(s) – a brief professional background including your qualifications and anything which distinguishes you from the competition
- a phone number.

Your brochure may also show:
- a photograph of you and/or your treatment room
- a map or directions if you choose to give a work address
- testimonials from satisfied clients
- your hours of work
- details of your fees
- approximate length of consultation
- your policy on charging for cancellations
- a convenient time to phone you.

Many people embarking on careers in complementary therapies have come from a completely unrelated background or have just completed their full-time education. How do you show that you are competent when this is all new to you?

In fact, if you look back over your life to date, you may well find something which links your past and present careers. Perhaps you have had experience in dealing with certain groups of people such as the elderly or the young. For example:

■ Mary Jones trained as a massage therapist once her children started school. Her experience of dealing with fraught mothers and their offspring led her to take further training in both pregnancy and baby massage. In addition to her practice she now runs classes in these at the XYZ Health Centre.

■ Paul Green was a violinist with a London orchestra. He became interested in complementary therapies when dealing with the aches and pains brought about by his professional life. This led him to train as a massage therapist and his former colleagues now benefit from his new skills.

■ Joanna Brown has just completed her full time education and recently qualified as a beauty therapist. She has always taken pride in her own appearance and her interest in clothes and makeup led her to set up her own business. She is currently undertaking further training as a colour analyst.

■ Sally Marsden was an international dressage rider until she retired two years ago. During her successful career, she saw the benefits of Buqi for her horses and was inspired to train as a practitioner herself. In addition to a busy dressage teaching schedule, she now offers Buqi for horses and riders.

Most of us progress through several leaflets or brochures, reflecting the changes as our practice grows and develops. I felt at a loss when designing my first brochure, but soon began to enjoy writing about my great passion – massage. If you are enthusiastic about your therapy, others will pick up on that and will want to know more. Ask someone you know to read your draft and give constructive comments before finalising the text. You may think that it is wonderful, but a good friend can always improve it!

Having decided on the content, you will have to choose how you will produce your brochure. The advent of desktop publishing and the home computer may enable you to produce something yourself, though using your own desktop facilities for print runs of 1,000 or more can be expensive and time consuming. It may be better to use a local photocopying facility or a quality printer. The choice will probably be determined by whether you choose to include a photograph or graphics and the quality of the paper or card that you wish to use for your brochure.

Some pitfalls to avoid in brochures are:
- spelling mistakes
- poor grammar
- giving too much information, which may discourage the reader
- an imbalance between the amount of information on the therapy and on the therapist
- poor quality paper/colour/print
- too much information on potential side effects/reactions to the therapy

BUSINESS CARDS

Business cards are cheaper to produce than brochures and are useful where you make personal contact with potential clients. They are easy to put away safely in a wallet, a purse or handbag, but are less effective when left out for people to pick up. They can double as an appointment card, although it may cost more to print both sides. However, if you have spoken to a person about your therapy and its potential benefits, a business card is a useful reminder. It may also be passed on easily by someone who is recommending you to a friend.

Business cards should give:

- your name
- qualifications
- types of therapy
- telephone number and address (or part if you are worried about your own safety)
- email/website addresses if you have them.

THE LAW AND YOUR BUSINESS STATIONERY

As well as looking professional, your stationery should also comply with a number of legal requirements.

If you are a sole trader or a partner in a partnership, the law states that your stationery must clearly display your business name, your own (personal) name (if different from your business name) and your business address on *all* your business stationery – letters, orders, cheques, payments, invoices, receipts, and so on.

These details don't have to be printed – you can handwrite them (although doing so isn't likely to convey the professional image you should be aiming for!) – but they must be easy to see and read.

If you are trading as a limited company, then the rules are very similar. You must show your company name on all your stationery, show the company's registered office address, company number and place of registration on all business letters and order forms, and include your company name, number, and registered office address on all business emails.

As far as the law is concerned, regardless of whether you are a sole trader, partnership or company, you should note that 'stationery' also includes your website, if you have one. If you do, then somewhere on your site (not so hidden away that no one will ever find it!) you must display your business name, address, email address, and VAT registration number (if you have one), and details of any relevant professional body that you belong to and/or any authorisation scheme which your service comes under.

TOOLS OF THE TRADE

Your equipment says louder than words whether you are committed to being totally professional. High quality, sturdy, effective equipment will instil confidence in your clients and provide greater comfort for you. As you intend to spend many years using your equipment, you should buy it with the aim of making your working life as comfortable as possible.

It is important to buy equipment that is as good a quality as you can afford. It may be that your training school has made some recommendations. If not, the internet has made researching much easier. There is also a list of suppliers at the end of this book.

CHOOSING A COUCH

If you are planning to buy a couch, it is essential to seek specialist advice. After all, this will be a major purchase for your new business. You expect to spend many hours working at your couch and that it will last you a long time. It must look professional, be sturdy and strong, and be the appropriate height, weight and material for you and the therapies you intend to offer. If you plan to offer additional therapies in future, remember that your couch must be suitable for those as well. Having a vision of what you intend your business to become will help you make an intelligent choice and save you money, as you'll avoid having to replace your couch because it no longer suits your needs. The best treatment in the world is ineffective if the client does not feel secure and comfortable on the couch. Equally, you cannot give an excellent treatment if the couch is not exactly right for you.

The choice can seem overwhelming, with considerable differences in quality and durability. There are several showrooms where you can see and try out different couches before you buy. Making the right decision is vital, so it is well worth the time and effort required to visit one, rather than risk buying such a major piece of equipment without seeing it first. Health exhibitions are also good places to look at a lot of products under one roof and ask advice from suppliers. It is worth lying down on a couch and asking someone else to lie on it before you buy it, to assess how comfortable it would be for you and your clients. One you have bought a couch, it is too late to learn that the face hole is in the wrong place, or that the height is not right for you.

Some companies offer start-up reductions for newly qualified therapists. Even if there is nothing advertised as such in their details, it is always worth asking. You could also ask your training school if they have an arrangement with a particular supplier. It is worth shopping round anyway, as your training school may themselves receive a discount from a supplier. There is a list of reputable suppliers at the end of this book.

Your choice will be largely governed by whether or not your couch is to remain in one place or needs to be portable. A hydraulic or electric couch is ideal if you have premises or a dedicated room to work from. I have a three-section hydraulic couch which gives me great flexibility in working and helps me conserve energy. I can change the height of the couch several times during a treatment, raise or lower the head and feet, and make it into a chair, which is ideal for those clients who would otherwise struggle to get on and off it. It also has a face hole and double thickness padding. Its dynamic load (i.e. the weight it will bear in the central section) is great enough for the heaviest client. The disadvantage of these types of couch is that they are extremely heavy, so they are only suitable for those lucky enough to have a dedicated work space.

The supporting structure of portable couches can be of aluminium, wood or carbon fibre. Aluminium is generally lightweight but rigid. It may also have push button adjustment. Carbon fibre is very lightweight but extremely expensive, though it looks lovely, as does wood.

When choosing your couch the following points should be considered:

- a portable couch must be light enough (no more than 15kgs) to carry comfortably and be fast and easy to put up and take down
- speed of set-up is important if you are mobile. A cable mechanism can be set up from suitcase to table in under seven seconds
- ensure your couch will adjust to the correct height for you and will close when set at that height. Your hip should be level with the top of the foam-filled vinyl
- check that a portable couch will fit easily into your car if necessary
- check the strength and stability of the couch to ensure it is suitable for your practice, particularly if you intend to do vigorous massage or deep bodywork. Look for impact strength to be 450lbs (208 kgs) and above, for massage

- choose the width that will suit you best; the most popular are between 26 and 28 inches. Wide couches are more comfortable for the client but more difficult for you to work at
- if you are taking your couch out a lot, it may be worth buying a protective carry case
- do not buy a fixed height couch unless it is made to your specifications
- do you need a tilting section? These can add 2-3kgs in weight
- do you need a face hole or face cradle? The advantages of a face cradle far outweigh the disadvantages of weight and additional expense
- if you need to be able to sit comfortably at either end, consider choosing Reiki End Panels but check whether this will affect the stability of your table
- is a hydraulic or electric couch suitable? Hydraulic/ electric couches cannot be stored away easily but are excellent for the therapist
- choose an appropriate composition and thickness of foam filling. They should be flame retardant
- portable couches are easier to store
- do you plan to train in any additional therapies? If so, choose a couch that is suitable for them all.

(written with assistance from Spencer Randon of *Therapy Essentials*)

TOWELS AND COUCH COVERS

It is not necessary for items such as your couch covers, towels and accessories to match, though you may prefer it. You could save some money by buying towels that are 'seconds' or from a market. There are also specialist companies that sell towels for professional use. I think it is essential to have towels for professional use only; keep them separate from your domestic towels. Be cautious about whatever you use to wash them in; many clients dislike strong smells and it may be unpleasant combined with essential oils.

Towels soon become worn if you use oils in your treatment and need fairly regular replacement. Once they are too worn for professional use, what do you do with them? I keep my local vets and riding stables supplied with towels: they are ideal for animals.

Couch covers are available in a range of widths, fabrics, and colours. Some companies offer student 'start-up' kits consisting of a couch cover, face ring, and covered pillow. This saves a little money when compared with buying each item individually.

Paper couch rolls will help protect your couch covers and provide a clean surface for each client. If you are unable to store a whole box, consider sharing one with a colleague. Some hairdressing and beauty suppliers sell rolls singly, though this can be more expensive.

BASE OILS, ESSENTIAL OILS AND WAXES

There is a good choice of companies selling both organic and non-organic base oils and essential oils. It is worth setting up a therapist's account with one or more. Most have two price lists, one professional and one for the public. In order to qualify for a trade account you will need to provide proof of your professional status by sending them a copy of your qualification certificate. You can usually order online and, over a certain amount, delivery is usually free. You could consider sharing an order with a colleague to save on delivery costs.

Base oils have different properties and 'slip'. It is worth trying a small amount of several kinds until you decide on a favourite.

Fractionated coconut, almond, grapeseed and sunflower are all good base oils. Avocado, jojoba, wheatgerm and apricot are more expensive and are not so commonly used on a daily basis. Waxes are less messy, and although they take some getting used to, are popular with therapists doing bodywork.

Selling goods

Many therapists sell ancillary products such as oils, beauty products and nutritional supplements. Doing so can increase your income but you will create a need for further storage space. There are some additional issues which you will need to consider, too.

If you make your own products – such as blends of oils, body lotions, or face creams – make sure you are aware of any legislation you need to comply with. In the examples just given, for example, the products themselves must comply with the Cosmetic Products (Safety) Regulations 2004 and/or the General Product Safety Regulations 2005, and there are strict requirements about labelling, too. If you are not sure about what legislation applies to your products, start by asking Trading Standards and get further professional legal advice if necessary. Getting it wrong could land you with a hefty fine and a lawsuit against you.

If you have a regular order of products from a supplier, which you then sell on to your clients and the public, it is advisable to have a contract in place between you. This should set out the essential details of the arrangement between you and the supplier – such as about when payment is due, when the products become legally yours (e.g. on delivery, or on payment?), and what recourse you have if the products are faulty or the wrong quantity is delivered, and so on. Making sure you have these eventualities covered from the start may well save you money, time, and hassle later on.

Finally, you will need robust insurance cover (see also Chapter 1). If you are selling products to the public, this is an absolute must. If you sell your own products, and they harm or injure someone, you are strictly liable at law, which means that an injured person can sue you – and is entitled to compensation – without having to prove any negligence on your part. All they have to prove is that they were injured or made ill, and that your product was the cause.

This obviously means that you are taking on considerable risk if you decide to sell your own products, so it makes sense to take out product liability insurance. You should aim to obtain cover of at least £1M.

CHECKLIST

- ❏ have you set a realistic budget for your practice?
- ❏ have you arranged a business telephone?
- ❏ do you have money available to buy the necessary equipment?
- ❏ have you chosen your equipment with thought and care?
- ❏ do you have all the equipment needed to give a treatment?
- ❏ do you have your personalised stationery printed?
- ❏ have you made arrangements for laundering couch covers, towels, etc?
- ❏ have you set up trade accounts with some suppliers?

4 BECOMING PROFESSIONAL

It is the capacity to care that give life its deepest significance.
PABLO CASALS, CELLIST

INITIAL CONTACT WITH THE CLIENT

The telephone is often your client's initial contact with you. Keep the following points in mind when dealing with client phone calls:

- by your telephone manner you will encourage or discourage potential clients
- the initial call provides your main opportunity to decide if this caller is someone you wish to treat
- you can learn a lot by the caller's manner towards you
- you need to decide if it is appropriate for you to treat individual callers, or whether they should be referred elsewhere
- by taking some of the case history over the phone you may not need to spend so much time on it when the client comes to you
- it is better to allow the potential client to leave a message and return their call later than to under-sell yourself when caught at an inconvenient time

Your voicemail or answering message should be business-like and impersonal, but still welcoming. Do not give any description of yourself. You should state clearly what you offer in your practice, even if this involves stating that you do not offer any sexual services. Genuine clients should not be put off if you explain this. It is better to be straight on the phone than risk an embarrassing or dangerous situation face to face.

Obtain as much information as possible from your client, e.g. name, address and phone number. If you are uncertain that the caller is genuine, you can check by calling them back to ask for further information for your records. Ask where the caller heard of you (this also helps you evaluate the value of your advertising) and why s/he needs treatment.

If something about the caller rings your alarm bells, make an excuse not to treat them, however much you need the money. Be polite, firm, and avoid being drawn into discussion.

If you make an appointment, but are still unhappy about someone coming to a clinic or your home for the first time, either ensure you are not alone with them or ask a friend or colleague to phone you after a certain time while the client is still there. Arrange a code to indicate to your friend whether or not you are safe. You can arrange the same if you are the one making the visit.

MOBILE PHONES

Many therapists now use a mobile number for their business. This may be easier and/or cheaper than having a land line but you will need to consider how you will separate your work and private life. Unless you have two mobile phones, clients may call you when you do not wish to answer their calls. I rarely use my mobile phone for work as I only want to take calls from clients when I have access to my diary. A colleague finds using his mobile helpful, as if a client asks for a treatment at short notice, he says he is away from home whether he is or not.

Email

It may also be convenient to communicate by email, but most clients will want to speak to you before booking their first appointment. Email is more useful when you know a client. It is also a convenient way to pass on relevant information to them, for example, something you promised to look up for them.

If you use email, be careful how you do so, particularly where first-time or potential (rather than existing) clients are concerned. Under relatively new (2003) legislation, it is a criminal offence to send email spam to someone.

What counts as 'spam'? Put very simply – anything that someone hasn't asked for. If you email your clients about their forthcoming appointment, that's fine. If you bombard them with information about your sideline chocolate business, then that will be spam, because it is not related to your therapy business. Similarly, don't send emails about what you offer to anyone who hasn't indicated a specific interest about your services. But if you've had a chat with someone at, say, a networking event, and they've indicated their interest in your services and have given you their contact details, then that's probably ok. But you must always allow them to opt out from receiving future emails from you, and you must make it clear how they can do that.

Care of the client
and the first treatment

You should have already learned the basic principles of the care of your client in the course of your training. However, it is such an important aspect of your practice that it is worth reminding ourselves of the following:

- be welcoming and make your client feel at ease
- provide reassurance as to the nature of your treatment
- keep your client covered to maintain their dignity as much as possible
- be sensitive to your client's needs
- offer the use of a toilet
- offer water or a hot drink as appropriate
- establish whether there are any possible contraindications to your treatment
- take a case history
- be aware that your client may not disclose sensitive information at the first session
- explain why you need to ask potentially intrusive questions
- discuss their expectations of the treatment
- explain what will happen during your treatment
- agree a treatment plan or course of action and give an estimate of the number of times the client may need to see you

In practice, your care of your client extends beyond the treatment room. They need your care as much before and after the treatment as during it. Do your utmost to make them feel safe, valued and well cared for.

However much you think you have explained clearly to a client what happens in a session, they may be anxious until they know you better. It is your job to reassure them and talk them through what you are doing. I tell my clients that if they tell me there is something they specifically don't like during a treatment I will stop doing it. No client should feel that they are at your mercy, or enduring some sort of package deal because you have not realised that they are uncomfortable about your treatment.

When you have finished treating your client, leave them alone for a while to 'come round'. Offer water and make sure that they are safe to drive before allowing them to leave. It is good practice to ask them if they would like to book another appointment. This is not being 'pushy'– it is part of providing a further service to them. It is much easier to change an appointment than make one from scratch. Many clients will keep meaning to call you but wait until they are in crisis, which means you have to work harder on them to achieve even a small improvement. You are not working in their best interests by allowing this to happen. If you have not seen them for a while, you could send a reminder by email or phone, though this puts the responsibility back onto you.

You should also give your client a realistic expectation of the number of treatments you think they will need. When someone first sees me I may need to treat them weekly, but as their condition improves their visits become further apart until they reach a maintenance stage. Even if you are not giving a course of treatments, you should suggest to the client when it would be a good idea to see you again.

TERMS AND CONDITIONS

Much of client care comes down to managing expectations. The more information the client has about what they can expect from you before, during, and after their treatment, the happier they are likely to be. Similarly, it helps both of you if they know what you expect of them. Examples might be that if they want to cancel an appointment, they let you know as soon as possible. Or that you take payment only in cash or by cheque. If your client doesn't know how you operate, and what your 'ground rules' are, then the chances of an awkward situation arising are high.

One way of managing expectations is to have a set of terms and conditions for your clients to read before they come to you for treatment – and preferably even before they make a firm booking with you. It doesn't have to be long or formal – it just needs to set out simply and clearly, how you work, what your client can expect, and what you expect of them.

Payment and cancellation provisions are particularly important. This is your chance to tell it how it is! For example, you might include how long a treatment will last, how long before an appointment they should arrive and so on. Don't fudge the issue when it comes to payment. You cannot beat around the bush when dealing with the subject of money if you want to succeed in business. Just say what you want to say in clear language. Here is a very simple example of a payment clause:

- The price of your treatment is to be paid by you to me in full at the end of your treatment by cheque or cash, unless otherwise agreed in advance between us.

The sentence says exactly what it needs to. It may not be the prettiest prose ever, but it's clear, and should prevent any misunderstandings. You don't have to opt for full payment on the day of course – you can always ask for a deposit in advance (particularly if it is a first-time client), and the rest on the day, or whatever other arrangement suits you.

Similarly, be clear about your cancellation policy. You could consider writing something along these lines: 'Any appointment cancelled or postponed by you within 24 hours of the scheduled start time, or any non-attendance by you at an appointment, will be deemed a late cancellation, and I reserve the right to charge you the full price for the appointment accordingly.'

Other areas you might want to address include whether you will charge a deposit, that you have the right to refuse a booking at your sole discretion, what happens if the client turns up late, by what method you accept payment (e.g. cash, cheque, PayPal or similar, or BACS), what will happen if *you* become ill and need to cancel their appointment – I'm sure you can think of others. Even seemingly trivial things, like asking that you require your client to turn off his or her mobile phone while having a treatment, is worth putting in your terms. That way, both of you know exactly where you stand, and there is little scope for misunderstanding.

It is worth printing your terms and conditions (or an abbreviated version of them) in your brochure, and displaying them on your website if you have one. If you display them on your website, make sure they are not buried on an obscure page which no one will ever find! Transparency is what you are aiming for – you're trying to make your relationship with your clients easier, not more difficult.

You can also put a 'medical' disclaimer in your terms of the kind you have probably come across during your training. This should state that the client understands that you are not medically qualified, that they should not cease or alter conventional treatment or medication for any reason without consulting their doctor, and that whatever treatment you give them is not a diagnosis, prescription, treatment or cure for any disease or a substitute for professional medical care.

(Finally, bear in mind that if you are treating anyone under the age of 18, they are not legally of an age in which they can enter into a contract – which is what they would be doing if they agreed to your terms. You will therefore need to get their parent or guardian's agreement instead.)

KEEPING CLIENT RECORDS

Keeping detailed records of your treatments is part of your duty of care to your clients. They are also a means of protecting yourself should anyone make a complaint against you. They must be clear, factual and legible records of each treatment that you give. Your clients are legally entitled to read their records, so do not write anything which you would not want them to see. If you make a mistake, cross it out but do not use Tippex, and leave it visible.

You may want to ask your client about their diet, lifestyle and the amount of alcohol they consume, or if they take recreational drugs. There is a fine line between taking a case history and what the new client may feel is the Spanish Inquisition. It may be better to tease this information from them gradually and add it to your records as you can, rather than risk your client experiencing your questioning as intrusive.

You should record what you did during the treatment and whether the client reported any response or reaction to it, or to the previous session. If you sell the client any products or supplements or recommend another therapist, you should record this, too.

Many people are poor historians. I ask all the pertinent questions. "No," they reply, "I haven't had recent surgery." I then find a large livid scar, and when questioned they say "Oh, that was my coronary artery bypass graft. I had it two months ago." Or having said they have no musculo-skeletal problems, they'll get off the couch asking "Do you think this will help my bad back?"

I have been asked a couple of times by solicitors to give information to support clients claiming damages after a road traffic collision or when they have sued their employer. I would not have been able to remember the details of dates, number of treatments, progress of treatment, had I not kept such detailed records.

I have also been able to help a client assess the rate of growth of a 'suspect' mole. The first time I noticed it I recorded its approximate size and shape. When she was sufficiently concerned to see her GP, my records provided details on how much it had grown and how quickly.

Remember that you could be asked to produce your client records in a court of law. A solicitor asked me to send a copy of my notes for a client who was suing her employer for sexual harassment. The very first thing I had written was 'stressed at work'. If you are asked to release records in this way, you must ask the client for their permission before doing so. In that case, the solicitor had enclosed the client's written consent with his request.

You might want to consider mentioning the circumstances in which you will be obliged to release the client's records in your terms and conditions or disclaimer. That way the client will be made aware that it is your legal duty to release his or her records in certain situations, and may help you avoid an awkward discussion later on.

STORING YOUR RECORDS

Record keeping is a vital part of good practice – no matter who your clients are. If your clients are in the care of others (e.g. because they are vulnerable adults), you may have additional reporting responsibilities, but your record keeping should always be of the best possible standard.

You are almost certainly subject to the Data Protection Act (DPA) too. But do you know what that entails? If not, make it your business to do so – failure to comply with the DPA is a criminal offence and is punishable by a fine of up to £5,000.

The aim of the DPA, assisted by the Information Commissioner, is to protect the individual's right to privacy regarding how their personal information is handled. So if you hold anyone's – and that may mean suppliers and employees or freelancers, as well as clients – personal information electronically, or in an organised way on paper, you must comply with the DPA.

Formally speaking, there are two things you need to do. First, decide whether you need to register (called 'notification') as a 'data controller' – someone who holds personal information – with the Information Commissioner. If so, you must also provide details of how you use the information.

You will almost certainly need to notify if you hold client records

- electronically, i.e. on a computer, and/or on a CD, and/or
- on paper, in a 'structured' manner (e.g. in alphabetical order), so that someone could easily find information about a client. An example would be a card index, or a file of consultation forms.

Second, you must adhere to a few simple principles. The main ones are that the information must be: fairly and lawfully processed; processed for a specified purpose; adequate, relevant and not excessive; accurate and, where necessary, kept up to date; processed in line with the rights of the individual; and kept secure. It must not be kept for longer than is necessary.

Keeping your records secure is crucial. Have you done everything to prevent a break-in where your records are kept? If you keep records on computer, do you regularly back them up? Are your anti-virus software and firewalls up to date? Think through all the possible security threats.

You may also be collecting others' information if you have a website – particularly if it uses cookies. If so, have a readily visible privacy policy on your website telling users what information you collect, and how you use it.

But don't just guess whether the DPA applies to you – contact the Information Commissioner's office to find out for sure. The fee for notifying is currently £35, payable annually. Yes, it's more money out of your budget – but by adopting these simple measures and adhering to the requirements of the DPA, you'll avoid a possible criminal record, a fine, and client claims against you!

But it's also good business sense to process personal records properly. People are increasingly sensitive about how their information is handled. If you can show your business is DPA compliant, you'll improve your clients' confidence in you. Having properly organised records also helps you run your business efficiently. Lost, mislaid, or out-of-date records only waste your time and money.

The contact details for the Information Commissioner's office are at the end of this book. If you have any questions about notifying, or about any aspect of your responsibilities under the Act, get in touch with the Information Commissioner's office by telephone. They're there to help you!

In summary, records:

- provide the client's contact details

- provide the client's medical history
- are a useful way of charting progress (people often forget the symptoms they came with, and their improvement can be shown once the symptoms have disappeared)
- can record something we want to do or pick up on next session
- are useful for recording how often someone cancels or forgets
- are essential to look back on in the event of a complaint, as you won't remember everything about each client

Records should contain at least the following:
- name, address, and telephone number
- age or date of birth
- brief medical history, including any operations
- any medication
- GP's name and address
- reason for treatment
- symptoms at first consultation
- treatment plan
- date of each treatment

CONFIDENTIALITY

The Chambers Twentieth Century dictionary defines 'confidential' as 'given in confidence' and confidence as 'trust in secrecy, admission to knowledge of secrets or private affairs'. What does this actually mean to us as therapists? There are two points. One is that confidentiality refers to personal details which you should not reveal to anyone. I do not record information on such things as sexual abuse, violent relationships or rape. I write something which will remind me, but nothing which could be understood by anyone else.

The second point relates to the patient's medical condition. It is sometimes helpful to discuss case histories with colleagues or other health professionals for the greater good of the patient. Needless to say, the patient should not be named. If, however, you need to identify them (for example, if you needed to discuss their treatment with their GP, or other therapist) you must ask for the client's prior written permission. Even then, you might expect to discuss Miss Smith's bad back, but not that she is currently in a violent relationship, even if you think this is relevant.

While on the subject of confidentiality, I have been asked how I feel about therapists using celebrity endorsement. It might seem a good idea to be able to endorse your business with a comment by someone famous whom you have treated. If you wish to do that, you must ask their permission first. My own experience of treating well-known people is that what they value most is the fact that no one knows that I treat them.

Checklist
- ❑ have you checked whether you need to register with the Information Commissioner?
- ❑ have you organised safe storage of your records?
- ❑ have you drawn up your terms and conditions?
- ❑ have you adopted a professional mindset?

5 MAKING A NAME FOR YOURSELF

The gods only go with you if you put yourself in their path.

ARISTOTLE

NAMING YOUR PRACTICE

Some therapists like to give their business a name. This can be a good idea, but think carefully about the image you want to create. The name may mean one thing to you and quite another to someone else. For example, Margaret wanted to call her business Wilderness Therapies. She saw that as somewhere lovely, quiet and serene. However, her clients may associate that with something overgrown and uncared for, or with religious images of Christ in the wilderness. John called his business Body Positive. He received a lot of phone calls from clients who thought he specialised in treating people who are HIV positive. He was happy to treat them, but it wasn't the image he had intended to create. While you can't control how people will respond to your practice, you should think about possible word associations.

Make sure, too, that you don't use a name that someone else is already using, particularly if they live in the same region as you and also work in the complementary health field. In a worst-case scenario, they could sue you! A quick check of your local phone directories and the internet should be all you need to do to confirm that you're not stepping on anyone else's toes.

ADVERTISING

As you will now understand, unfortunately people will read into your advert what they choose to see, which is not necessarily what you have written. All general advertising of complementary therapies carries the risk of attracting nuisance calls. You therefore have to be extremely careful how you word your advert to avoid any misunderstanding. Words such as 'service', 'caring', 'personal', 'friendly', 'mature', 'enjoy', and even 'Swedish' are often misconstrued. At all costs, I would avoid using the word 'relief', even if it is preceded by 'stress'. Further, any reference to personal appearance is not relevant to anyone seeking genuine complementary therapies.

Words conveying a professional image include 'treatment', 'alleviate', 'clinical', 'therapy', 'qualified', 'appointment' and 'therapist'.

Newsagent or Post Office
An inexpensive way of advertising is to place a postcard in your local newsagent or Post Office. As long as it is worded very carefully, it can bring you valuable local clients for a small outlay.

Local paper
If you pay for an advertisement in your local paper, particularly if you take one on a regular basis, they may be prepared to give you editorial space. You will normally be expected to write your own article, but remember they will edit it, particularly the last paragraph. They are keen to attract regular advertisers and may offer you discounts or special rates. There is no harm in asking, anyway. For some reason boxed adverts attract fewer nuisance calls, so it is worth bearing this in mind. My local paper agreed to instigate a new advertising column, Natural Therapies, when a group of therapists asked for it. When space permitted, they printed a note at the top of the column indicating that all therapists advertising in that section were qualified and genuine.

Yellow Pages and Thomson's Guide

Although these advertisements are comparatively expensive, they can be a reasonable source of new clients. You should advertise in the Complementary or Alternative Health section. They also have online directories, for which you have to pay an additional amount.

The directory staff are themselves usually aware of the problems associated with advertising complementary therapies and will do their best to help you produce a professional advert. They also offer a choice of payment options so you don't have to find all the money in one go. Advertising in the directories gets your name out into the public domain and shows you are committed and serious about your business.

The disadvantage of advertising in these, other than the financial outlay, is that other companies use them to approach you about yet more advertising. You are likely to have more calls offering you advertising space than are welcome.

Websites

Many therapists now have their own websites. Only you can decide how important a website is in your early days as a therapist. My own view is that if I were looking for a therapist I would try to obtain a personal recommendation first, though I would look at a therapist's website to find out more before booking a session with them. Your website can be an effective shop window but it may not directly bring you much business. Depending on your IT skills (or lack of them), you may want to look for specialist help in this area. There are also many online directories which you can consider listing yourself in, whether or not you have a website yourself. Most training schools have a section on their website for finding a local practitioner, so make sure you are listed on yours.

SETTING UP AND RUNNING
YOUR OWN WEBSITE

There are a number of companies that specialise in helping complementary therapists set up and maintain their own websites at a reasonable cost. Some offer a free trial to help you decide whether this suits you or not. Some may help you gain a place high in the listings by suggesting key words (a process called search engine optimisation) and ways of setting up your site to best effect. They will also typically give you feedback on visitor numbers to each page of your site.

Alternatively, you may wish to pay someone to set up and look after the site for you. One disadvantage of that, as I discovered to my cost, is that should they 'go bust', it is difficult to regain control of your site and it may take you a while to discover that your website is no longer available. If you get someone to create (and/or maintain) your website for you, try to put in place an agreement in writing between you. This should cover, at minimum, when you will pay (this may be e.g. by deposit and then instalments, or the full amount on completion of the website), what exactly you expect your website builder to do, and what will happen in the event that they don't finish the work (e.g. that, if they haven't done so already, they should hand over to you the work done to date, and all rights to the domain name and content, and perhaps also the source code. The latter may enable someone else to finish the project for you with minimum delay).

If you think you want to get someone to maintain and update your website for you, do be very clear at the outset as to the costs involved. This is never a cheap option, and a good website designer will be able to build you a site which you can easily update and edit yourself even if you don't have any previous 'techie' knowledge.

Keeping your site looking fresh and the content up to date is a vital part of creating a professional image of yourself and your business, so it is better not to tie yourself in to having to pay someone else to make lots of minor changes for you on a regular basis.

Your own website should include:
- 'about us'
- about the therapy
- testimonials
- FAQs
- contact details.

TARGETING A PARTICULAR MARKET

Think about the kind of client you would like to treat. Where would they be likely to hear of you? Approach health clubs, swimming pools and leisure centres, golf clubs and anywhere else you can think of. If they don't have a vacancy for you to work there, ask to leave your brochures *and keep returning to top them up*. Be sure to always have copies of your brochure and/or business card in your wallet or handbag and your car.

You could also ask to leave them at:
- local chemists
- hairdressers
- dentists
- doctors' surgeries
- physiotherapy clinics
- osteopaths/chiropractors
- chiropodists
- library

- local pubs
- health food shops (N.B. many are only willing to accept a business card due to lack of space)
- New Age bookshops
- Citizens Advice Bureaux
- Environmental Health Departments at local councils
- Tourist Information offices

FREE TREATMENTS AND GIFT VOUCHERS

It is well worth offering a free treatment to other health professionals and those contacts who may recommend you. I once gave a free treatment to someone who then recommended me to a friend of hers. The friend passed my phone number to a lot of people and my business grew substantially as a result. It was really worth my while to give that free treatment. The important thing is that both you and the client are happy with the arrangement and that you do not feel taken for granted. Some choices are:

- give the first treatment free, then charge your normal fee
- give some free treatments as appropriate, but review the situation after you have given a few
- offer say, 12 treatments for the price of 10 (paid in advance).

It is also worth giving vouchers for treatment to local charities to raffle or auction. If the voucher is not taken up, you have lost nothing. Your name will be mentioned at the time of the raffle, which is good advertising for you and gives the impression that you are a generous, caring person! If someone takes up the voucher, you will give your time, but they will probably come back, and will tell their friends about you.

Talks to groups

Giving talks to groups such as National Childbirth Trust, Women's Institute, charities, luncheon clubs and the like is also an excellent way of getting your name known. In my experience, the more talks you give, the easier it becomes to do them. It is good to keep reaffirming your belief in your therapy and you may well gain new clients. Be careful not to make claims about your therapy or suggest that you can cure anyone. People will respect you more for being realistic about what you might achieve. You are unlikely to be paid much for giving talks, but you should be able to cover your expenses such as travel, parking, and if you have children, baby-sitting. Take plenty of business cards or brochures to hand out.

Radio talks

It is unlikely that you will be offered the chance to speak on the radio early in your career. However, it is worth calling a radio station if you have a particularly interesting idea. If you are offered an interview it is likely to be at very short notice – often the same day. It is therefore worth having a 'skeleton' talk or some questions and answers prepared in case.

As an alternative to your local radio station, a nearby hospital may have its own radio station. They may well like you to give a talk in which you may promote your own field of therapy but, in my opinion, it would be inappropriate to advertise yourself directly, unless invited to do so by the radio presenter.

It is natural to feel nervous about such a different environment, but usually the person conducting the interview will be encouraging, and do their best to put you at ease. The most daunting interview I gave was alone in a studio with my microphone, while the interviewer was a hundred miles away in another studio!

Take a blank CD with you so that you can have a recording of your talk. It is useful to know how often you said 'er', and how you could improve on it another time.

NETWORKING

With the best will in the world clients will not beat a path to your door if they don't know about you. Making contacts can be a very daunting prospect for most newly qualified therapists. However, there are things you can do to begin getting your business off the ground.

Make sure all your friends and work colleagues know what you do. Even if they don't come to you themselves, they may recommend you to others. Offer them some brochures to hand out to people that they know. Word of mouth is the best way of attracting clients, but it does take time. Remember to keep in touch with your training school. Many keep a register of therapists from which to give names to enquirers. I have also gained clients from sources such as:

- neighbours
- parents and staff at my children's school
- the stables where I ride
- the postman (who sent a colleague with a bad back)
- taxi drivers

OTHER HEALTH PROFESSIONALS

You could send an introductory letter to physiotherapists, doctors, dentists, osteopaths, chiropractors and chiropodists. Follow it up with a phone call to see if they would like any more information. You may like to offer them a free treatment so they can experience the benefits first hand. It is good to develop a link with a practice, as they may 'sell' you to their clients. A referral from another professional is more valuable than any amount of advertising.

You could also phone other therapists in your discipline (the phone book and local paper should provide these). Make friends with them and assure them that you don't want to tread on anyone's toes. Established therapists can be a helpful source of advice and may pass on work when they are able.

Contact other complementary therapists, too. Your local homeopath, herbalist, acupuncturist, psychotherapist, naturopath, and reflexologist may all be delighted to hear from you. They can also help you maintain your own health.

Years ago I organised a therapists' supper. About eight therapists of different disciplines came, bringing a dish to share, and their business cards. We had such a good evening we decided to make it a regular event. Not only are we all able to refer clients to one another, but we all gained enormously from the stimulation of discussion and mutual support.

Sending formal letters to other health professionals is discussed in Chapter 6. They are also a means of establishing contact and reputation with them. I once wrote to a GP after treating a lady I was unable to help. When another patient asked the doctor if he could recommend a massage therapist he looked up my letter in the first lady's notes and referred the new patient to me. My lack of success with his patient did not deter him from referring another one to me. Maybe it was my honesty in admitting I had not been able to help that made an impression on him.

CURRICULUM VITAE

Preparing a CV is a useful discipline whether you are setting up your own practice or seeking employment. It can help you to identify where your individual advantage might lie, for it is this which distinguishes you in the eyes of your client or prospective employer. Although I am self employed, I have also been asked for a summary of my professional life by doctors before they would refer patients to me.

Your CV should contain your

- name
- address
- phone number
- details of training, including any work experience you may have had in that time
- work experience, with the most recent first.

Checklist

- ❑ have you planned a marketing strategy?
- ❑ have you set an advertising budget?
- ❑ have you established some good contacts?
- ❑ have you contacted other therapists near you?
- ❑ have you prepared a 'skeleton' talk?
- ❑ have you decided where to advertise effectively?
- ❑ have you researched clubs and organisations where you can give a talk?
- ❑ have you prepared your CV?
- ❑ have you decided how many free treatments you are prepared to offer?
- ❑ do you need your own website?
- ❑ do you need to be listed in an online directory?
- ❑ are you listed on your training school's website?
- ❑ if you have named your business, have you chosen it with great care?

6 DEALING WITH OTHER HEALTH PROFESSIONALS

'Who steals my purse steals trash... but he that filches from me my good name robs me of that which not enriches him and makes me poor indeed.'   IAGO (*OTHELLO*, SHAKESPEARE)

DO AS YOU WOULD BE DONE BY

When you first start out in practice you may regard all other therapists as competitors. Just as you chose to adopt a mindset of becoming professional, you can also choose how you view other therapists. If other therapists are unfriendly towards you, that is their loss. If you come from a viewpoint that all other therapists are reducing your potential clientele, you are likely to be met with suspicion and dislike. If you expect friendliness and support, it is more likely that you will encounter just that.

Your training or professional body's code of conduct will have provided guidelines about how to behave towards your colleagues. These normally include not poaching other therapists' clients and not criticising colleagues and competitors.

Cooperation over working hours and sharing supplies can be mutually beneficial.

■ Theresa, an aromatherapist, wanted to have a stand at a local health exhibition but was put off by the cost. She spoke to John, a Reiki practitioner, who also wanted to be there. They were able to share the cost of a stand between them. The exhibition was quiet when it first opened, so they began by treating one another and people were soon attracted to their stand. They also met an osteopath they got on well with and agreed to refer clients to one another.

- Samantha is a newly qualified massage therapist. When looking through the phone book for other local therapists she discovers Martin, who lives and works nearby. Samantha calls Martin and they meet for coffee. Martin agrees to refer any clients to Samantha who would prefer to see a female therapist. Samantha cannot work after 4pm as she has to collect her young son from school then. She offers to send clients who need appointments at the end of the day to Martin. Soon they are exchanging treatments and cooperating over holidays and working patterns. Between them they offer a better service than either could provide by themselves. They also benefit from mutual support and friendship.

- Peter is setting up a practice near a chiropractor's surgery. He arranges to give Tim, the chiropractor, a free treatment and is soon making and receiving referrals. Tim sends appropriate clients and the 'selling' is already done by the time they contact Peter. If Peter treats someone and believes they need a chiropractor, he refers them to Tim. Again, clients receive a more holistic service than if Peter and Tim were not cooperating.

- James works from a hairdresser's. He gets very upset when new therapists start work in the area. In fact, he has complained three times about other therapists 'taking' his work. Client 1 left him because he found it difficult to park near the hairdresser. Instead, he went to Bryony who worked at a clinic where it was easier to park. Client 2 also went to Bryony, as she preferred to see a female therapist. Client 3 moved away from the area. Do you think James is justified in complaining?

We have to accept that sometimes clients leave for perfectly sound reasons. On the other hand, we would be justified in complaining if another therapist had actually tried to entice our clients away from us. Therapy is a very personal business and it seems to me that if our clients are happy with the treatment they receive from us, they prefer to continue seeing us rather than go elsewhere.

THE MEDICAL PROFESSION

Your main contact with doctors and other health professionals is likely to be mostly by letter. Letters to all health professionals should be on headed notepaper (see also Chapter 3 on your business stationery and the law). Write the letter in such a way that the other professional is likely to read it. I suggest you avoid using terms such as auras, energy blocks and the like, keeping your terminology as down to earth as possible. You are less likely to be dismissed as a New Age weirdo and have a better chance of the recipient taking notice!

Remember that the client's GP remains responsible for his/her patient's care, so s/he will need to reassure themselves that you are competent. They may also prefer you to have some experience. Offering them a free treatment is a good way of introducing yourself. Be prepared to show some evidence of your training, such as your certificates and CV. They will also want to know that you are adequately insured.

If your letter relates to a particular patient, their name address and date of birth should be in bold after 'Dear Dr----'. You might like to remind the person you are writing to about the patient. For example:

Dear Doctor Smith

Penny White, 12 George Street, Halifax. DOB 4/11/50

I have now given several weekly massage/reflexology/reiki/ whatever treatments to this 59-year-old lady with rheumatoid arthritis. I have worked particularly on her painful feet, and the two swollen fingers on her left hand. I have carried out gentle passive joint movements to all her affected joints with the aim of improving her mobility.

She reports that she has less pain and is taking fewer analgesics. She is also able to take her dog for longer walks than previously. We are both pleased with her progress and I shall continue to treat her monthly from now on.

If you feel this is insufficient or would like further information, please do not hesitate to contact me.

Yours sincerely

As your business increases you may like to write as a matter of course to your client's GP, if the client is willing to allow you. A standard letter to doctors could be something like this:

Dear Doctor Bloggs

Fred Smith, 12 The Green, Cambridge. DOB 8/6/60

I write as a matter of professional courtesy to inform you that your above named patient has come to me for a course of ...... treatment.

.... can be beneficial in a number of complaints, particularly those which are stress related. However, if you feel that .... is contra-indicated for this person, or you would like further information, please do not hesitate to contact me.

Yours sincerely

You should always seek a GP or hospital consultant's permission if your client is suffering from a serious medical condition, or has had recent surgery. If in doubt, you could arrange the client's appointment far enough ahead for you to do this. You may be asked to provide a CV or some information to show that you are competent. If you feel that treating a particular condition is beyond your abilities, it is better to say so rather than to find yourself in a situation you are unhappy about. If you know other more experienced therapists you could refer the potential client to them instead. You could also seek advice from your training school, professional organisation or an experienced colleague.

I have treated patients with active cancer, after recent open heart surgery, after recent fractures, with severe neurological disease, and even with a steel 'halo' following a neck fracture. In these cases I usually obtain written consent, which I keep with the client's notes. Occasionally, I obtain verbal consent from either the GP or consultant and I record this in the patient's notes along with the date I spoke to them. You should also notify the doctor of your client's progress. This is courteous to the doctor, and gives him or her some idea of the efficacy of your therapy.

CHECKLIST

- ❑ are you observing your code of conduct in relation to working with fellow professionals?
- ❑ have you contacted other therapists in your area?
- ❑ have you thought about how you could cooperate with them?
- ❑ have you prepared a standard letter for doctors?
- ❑ have you obtained consent from a client's doctor where this is appropriate?
- ❑ do you have a ready-made consent form?
- ❑ have you thought of other ways to get yourself known?

7 DEALING WITH DIFFICULT SITUATIONS

A good head and a good heart are always a formidable combination. There are few misfortunes in this world that you cannot turn into a personal triumph if you have the iron will and the necessary skill. NELSON MANDELA

FIRST AID

There is nothing more frightening than a person collapsing in front of you, especially if you don't know what to do. If in doubt call 999. Even if your client recovers quickly, ambulance crews would rather attend and be sent away, than arrive too late because someone was reluctant to make an emergency call. However, a client's collapse may have absolutely nothing to do with the treatment you gave them. To put it in context, I have seen more people collapsing in the supermarket than I have in my treatment room. Occasionally I have had to provide plasters or dressings when a client has arrived with a recent minor injury.

Most complementary therapy training schools now insist that therapists take the one day 'Appointed Person at Work' course as a minimum. It is, in any case, useful to know how to resuscitate, deal with fainting, asthmatic attacks, epileptic seizures, and how to put someone who is breathing but unconscious into the recovery position.

You should have a basic First Aid kit in your treatment room if you work from home, which is clearly marked and easily accessible. You should keep it in a waterproof container and check and replenish it regularly. St John Ambulance and the British Red Cross recommend that it should contain:

- a variety of dressings and adhesives dressings
- tape
- bandages
- a triangular bandage
- tubular bandages
- disposable gloves
- cleaning wipes
- scissors
- safety pins
- gauze pads
- either a face shield or pocket mask for use in mouth-to-mouth resuscitation

If you run your own clinic, and employ staff, you must comply with the Health and Safety (First Aid) Regulations 1981. The Regulations require you to have 'adequate and appropriate' resources to ensure that first aid can be given to your employees (as well as clients, of course!) if they are injured or become ill.

What counts as adequate and appropriate (and this applies even to the contents of any First Aid kit you have on your premises) will depend entirely on your workplace and related circumstances – such as what kinds of risk there are on site. These may be minimal if you offer massage only, but if your services include acupuncture, or beauty treatments involving electronic equipment, then you can expect to make rather more provision. The obligation is on you to assess the risks yourself and take action accordingly.

For full details of what you need to do, visit the Health and Safety Executive's website, at www.hse.gov.uk.

DEFIBRILLATORS
If you work in a clinic there may be a defibrillator there for use in cases of cardiac arrest. If you own a clinic, I would recommend

buying a defibrillator and training all staff to use it. If someone collapses with a cardiac arrest, do you know what their chances of survival are? You may be shocked to know they are as little as 6%. However, if that person has swift access to early Cardio Pulmonary Resuscitation and defibrillation, their chances can increase to as much as 74%. It is therefore vital that you 'give it a go' to buy the person time before skilled help arrives.

Defibrillators are very easy to use. As you open the case, a voice tells you exactly what you must do: you simply follow the instructions. Defibrillators will not shock a heart which is functioning normally, so you will not do the person any harm.

MEETING YOUR CLIENTS' NEEDS

What do your clients need from you? First of all, they need to know that you are competent, professional, caring and work for their highest good. They need to be educated as to how you work, and given firm boundaries regarding things such as cancellations, arriving, leaving and paying on time. They need to know that you are there for them, that you value them but also that you have your own life.

I would also suggest that one of the client's greatest needs is for us to be gentle with them. We often don't know what has happened to people in their past and in my experience they do not reveal their distress immediately. Only once has someone walked into my treatment room and said "Hello, I'm Jenny, and I've been sexually abused." It is more usual for them to come for treatment for a long time (years rather than months) before saying anything. The same goes for those whose children have died, those who have been raped or those in violent relationships. Some people are very conscious of being overweight. ("I'll just lose another stone before I come to you"). Others have had traumatic experiences in the past which require gentle handling.

We need to be aware of our potential to hurt our clients unintentionally. If you insist that someone removes their underwear for a treatment and they have had a sexual trauma in the past, aren't *you* being abusive? I think it is better to give a less thorough treatment than cause a client such distress. If you have photos of happy children in your treatment room, could that upset a client whose child has died? And if a client is depressed, or dealing with a distressing situation, how would they feel about having a treatment from a relentlessly jolly therapist?

Remember, too, that a client may have suffered at the hands of another therapist. After I had given evidence in a crown court case against a colleague who was convicted of sexual assault, some of his victims said that they missed having massage, but felt too vulnerable to try again.

■ I went to a colleague, Mary, for a massage. I made it clear that I was tired and wanted to drift off during the treatment. I also said I was very upset, having just heard that a friend had been diagnosed with cancer. When I said he only had 15 years maximum to live, Mary's response was "That's good. Most people die of cancer much quicker than that!" She then spent the massage chatting, asking me about my husband's job, and telling me how sensitive she is.

Do not assume that clients want to talk about their problems and traumas during a treatment: there is also great value in being able to leave them on one side for a while. If you chat too much during the massage, you are taking your client's time rather than them taking yours. A certain amount of chat is fine, as your clients may want to get to know you. Just be aware that it may not always be what they want. Ask yourself if you are giving your time to the client or if they are giving their time to you. Remember that he who pays the piper should be calling the tune.

Apart from gentleness and acceptance, what else do our clients need? I believe those needs vary from treatment to treatment. Sometimes we need silence, sometimes to talk, sometimes a gentle rub, sometimes a vigorous workout. You should develop sensitivity to your client's needs over time. You can always reflect back your own perceptions, for example: "I sense you need a gentle massage today, is that right?" Ask open questions such as "How are you feeling?" "Is this what you want today?"

I remember having Alexander Technique lessons with a woman who (ab)used her clients. It was impossible to concentrate while she related the gruesome details of her abortion/divorce/violent relationship. Several of my friends had lessons from her, too, and we all had the same experience and the same tale of woe. She had no idea of what she was doing to her clients, even telling us off if we didn't get something right! (To be fair, I have since then had excellent Alexander lessons with other teachers.)

Sometimes outside influences prevent us from doing our best. One day I was treating a lady I'd been seeing for a couple of years. She was just confiding that she had been sexually abused by a relative when my new washing machine arrived unexpectedly. Fortunately, I was able to give her more time after it had been fitted.

On another occasion I treated someone when I was completely exhausted. The tears were pouring down my face by the end of the session. I was just about to say to my client that I thought she should not pay me for such a poor treatment when she said "That was one of the best massages you've ever given me. It was really grounded and calm." It would seem that even when we are feeling less than our best we can help others. I have talked to colleagues about this, and many have felt on occasion that a treatment they gave was no good. The client has then declared it excellent! I believe it may be because of our intention for our clients.

YOUR INTENTION FOR YOUR CLIENTS

There is usually a great depth of communication between the hands of the giver and the body of the receiver in sensitive body work, and this makes the intent of the giver profoundly important ... There needs to be a desire to help, to soothe, to ease.   LEON CHAITOW, 'BODY TONIC'

Why is it that some therapists are really good while others are merely average? I believe it is not just a matter of training, ability, and personality, but intention. To treat someone really well, it has to be our intention to make a *positive* difference to them.

The paradox is that our intention for a good outcome runs alongside a detachment from that outcome, and a lack of fixed idea of what that will be. In other words, we want the best for our clients without imposing on them our idea of what that best should be. This also extends to ourselves, in that we should intend to be caring, able, conscientious therapists. Florence Nightingale said that hospitals should do the sick no harm. I believe that the same goes for complementary therapists too.

DEMANDING CLIENTS

It is difficult when someone rings wanting treatment NOW. You will have to judge each situation on its merits and decide whether or not you are being taken for granted. Remember that inflammation and some acute conditions are contra-indications for complementary therapies. Your clients should also consult their doctor or osteopath as appropriate. They are usually grateful for advice such as taking painkillers and/or Arnica tablets, and using an ice pack or hot pack until the acute condition subsides. You have at least addressed their worry, even if you are not able to treat them at the time.

I was once phoned late on Christmas Eve by a man I'd never met who wanted a treatment NOW. He had ignored his condition, which had been getting worse for months, finally catching up with him at Christmas. As it happened I was waiting for a doctor to visit my child who was ill, so it was easy to say no. The man tried a few other numbers I gave him (not surprisingly without success) and came to me afterwards at a more convenient time.

Of course there will be occasions when you will be happy to put yourself out for your clients, but do think carefully about it first. You may have ambitions to heal the sick and change the world, but you cannot be effective 24 hours a day, 365 days a year. It is important to take regular holidays and to have enough rest yourself. After all, this is what you would probably advise your clients!

I usually say that massage is a strenuous job and they would not receive a good treatment from me at 11pm or whatever they have asked for. Or that if they had phoned at 2pm instead of 6pm, I could have seen them that day.

This is also where you can cooperate with other therapists. Find out when your colleagues are working, and let them know your hours. You can then help by giving each other's phone numbers if you are unable to treat someone.

Contra-indications to and Cautions with Treatment

It can be difficult to refuse to treat a demanding client, even when you know that a treatment is not in their best interests. However, it is important that you are firm in telling them exactly that. Many will not know whether they should attend for an appointment or not. Ask the following questions to help you come to a decision:

- do they have a fever? (if so, tell them to stay at home)
- are they infectious? (if they are, you don't want their germs)
- is there any possibility that a treatment could exacerbate their condition? (if so, defer the appointment)
- do they actually want to be touched? (if not, defer the appointment)
- are you prepared to risk contracting their bug?

It may be that you could treat them, avoiding a particular area of the body. If they have a medical condition such as cancer, you will need to obtain consent from their doctor before you treat them, or you may not wish to treat them at all. *It is vital not to exceed your competence and skills.* You can always refer them to a more experienced practitioner or contact your training school for advice. It is perfectly reasonable to tell a potential client that you want to take further advice before treating them. They will appreciate your professionalism and care.

Contra-indications vary from therapy to therapy, but the most common are:

- first trimester of pregnancy
- under the influence of drugs or alcohol
- infectious disease
- skin infection
- very recent surgery
- serious conditions such as cancer
- inflammation
- high temperature

To further protect yourself and to prevent misunderstandings with and complaints from clients, you should get your clients to agree to and to sign a disclaimer before you treat them. You can choose whatever wording you like, but make it absolutely clear that you are not a trained medical professional and that the client accepts full responsibility for their treatment.

For example:
- I will provide a massage/reflexology/whatever treatment to the best of my ability and, as far as reasonably possible, in accordance with the information provided by you. You understand and agree that I am not medically qualified and do not medically diagnose any condition or symptom, and that a massage/reflexology/whatever treatment is not intended in any way whatsoever as a diagnosis, prescription, treatment or cure for any disease or as a substitute for regular medical care.

And for the signature piece:
- I, [name of client], hereby consent to receiving a

massage/reflexology/whatever treatment. I have been made aware of the possible side-effects and take full responsibility for any consequences of the treatment.

Signed:
Date:

IF YOU HAVE TO CANCEL

For some unknown reason, many clients expect their therapist to be available, enthusiastic and healthy 24 hours a day, 365 days a year. Unfortunately we cannot get away from the fact that sometimes we have to let clients down. If we cancel because we are ill, we let them down, but we risk letting them down in an even worse way by passing on our germs to them. We may also extend the duration of our illness by working instead of resting.

If you are unable to work for any reason, be it holiday or illness, it is responsible and professional to suggest a colleague who can cover for you. If your clients prefer to wait for you, that is fine, but at least you have given them the choice. Some therapists voice concerns that their clients will desert them for whoever is covering. I can only say that I personally have never found this to be the case. I have passed my clients to colleagues during times of illness, holiday and maternity leave. My clients have been grateful for the opportunity to continue having massage. Those who have *not* had any treatment in the meantime have been the ones to get out of the habit.

If you do need to cancel appointments, you must be meticulous in ensuring that you contact those clients again afterwards. It is both poor business and poor care of your client to promise to contact them and not do so. It is your job to rearrange the appointment, not your client's to chase you up.

Nuisance phone calls

The most obvious thing to say about nuisance phone calls is that you do not have to listen to them! Most of us forget this when we pick up the phone and find ourselves with an obscene caller on the other end.

Aim to have separate business and private lines or mobile phone as soon as you are able. If this is not possible when starting out, do it as soon as you can. If you use a landline you may find it useful to have a phone which displays the caller's number.

If nuisance calls become frequent, when you answer the phone pause before you speak then just say "hello". Do not argue, get angry or emotional. Rest the phone off the hook and go away leaving the person talking. After a while, put the phone back on the hook *without* listening to hear if the caller is still there. If you know the number of the nuisance caller and have a BT phone, you can arrange to refuse calls from that number by ringing 0800 800 150. If you are a non-BT customer contact your phone provider for help.

There is a recorded British Telecom information service on 0800 666 700. You can obtain information from BT on dealing with nuisance calls by dialling 0800 661 441. You could also contact your local police community safety department. It is a criminal offence to make malicious calls and callers are liable to be prosecuted.

Erections during a treatment

Remember that an erection is a perfectly normal physiological response. There is no need to overreact, nor do you necessarily need to do anything about it. Defuse the situation with a one-liner – sympathetic or not as appropriate. A full bladder can cause what looks like an erection, so before you make a withering comment, remember the poor man may just be bursting for a pee!

CLIENTS WHO MAKE SEXUAL ADVANCES

From talking to my colleagues I believe this is a rare occurrence, though in 20 years I have had to deal with a couple of awkward situations. Although I found one incident unpleasant, I didn't feel physically threatened or unsafe. I ended the treatment as soon as possible and asked the client to leave. When he next called me, I told him that I would not treat him again and explained why. Despite his protestations that "it was only a bit of fun", I stuck to my guns, re-stated that I found it unpleasant and refused to see him again.

Another time I treated a man and did feel unsafe. It was entirely my own fault, as my alarm bells had been ringing from the moment he first phoned and I was foolish enough to ignore them. **If you are ever remotely unhappy about treating someone, make an excuse and do not see them.**

As it can be upsetting, you should be prepared in case it happens to you. Have a ready-made excuse, e.g. your husband/wife/partner is due home (even if you are unattached!). Do not compromise your professional integrity, however much you need the money. In fact, you may need to ask them to leave without them paying you. Provide yourself with a personal alarm or a panic button if you wish, or attend a martial arts or self-defence class to give yourself confidence.

RISK OF VIOLENCE

It is natural for therapists to be concerned about possible encounters with violent or threatening people, particularly when doing home visits. Some therapists avoid this issue by treating clients of their own sex only. I personally feel that it is a pity to reject those seeking genuine treatment because of some vague potential risk. A group of therapists near me got together with the police to discuss issues of personal safety. **Our conclusion was that the risk of violent confrontation is extremely rare.**

However, my experience above demonstrates how important it is that you follow your gut instinct when making appointments with new clients. If your alarm bells are ringing, make an excuse and refuse to see them. They will not know that you are not really fully booked, going on holiday or rushing to pick up your child from school. This is one occasion when you would be justified in saying you will call the person back when you are taking bookings again, then not doing so.

In the unlikely event that you find yourself in a difficult situation, remember the following:

- if possible, arrange beforehand for someone to phone or call at a pre-arranged time
- stay calm and defuse the situation rather than get angry
- do not compromise your professional integrity
- talk it through with a colleague afterwards
- learn from the experience and evaluate your handling of it.

In my experience, if a man gives his name and phone number, he is genuine. Those seeking sexual services do not give their name, but enquire about the 'massage service.' You will soon learn to distinguish between the two. Occasionally I have stressed the fact that I do not provide sexual services only to have some poor chap say "I'm gay," or "But I've only got a bad shoulder!" However, it is better to risk offending a potential client than end up in a situation you could have avoided. Genuine enquirers will understand your position.

CLIENTS WITH POOR HYGIENE

Occasionally you will encounter a patient who has a real problem with their personal hygiene. Anyone can be a bit sticky on a hot day. If they comment on it themselves, offer the opportunity to wash or give them freshening wipes. Likewise, dirty feet can be cleaned with a baby wipe. A tactful way of dealing with this is to suggest that taking a shower or a long soak in the bath before they come to you will increase the benefit of your treatment.

REACTIONS TO TREATMENT

Those people used to allopathic medicine may be uncomfortable with the idea that it is possible to feel worse before feeling better. As we never know how someone will respond to treatment, it is worth mentioning to them that some form of reaction is perfectly normal. It is possible to do this without causing undue alarm to your clients.

Some useful remedies for dealing with reactions to treatment are:

- Arnica tablets for stiffness
- drinking lots of water to help excrete by-products of metabolism
- Rescue Remedy or Five Flower essence if they feel shaky
- reassurance
- a warm bath and a good night's sleep

CANCELLATIONS

Unless you are to suffer a great deal of inconvenience and sudden drops in income, it is essential to have a policy on cancellations. I experienced a lot of short notice cancellations until I told all my clients that I reserved the right to charge for them. You will soon get to know who is taking you for granted, and you are likely to feel resentful towards them unless you take action. It is your responsibility to educate your clients as to how you like to be treated. If you have several cancellations in a short period of time, you will lose a substantial amount of income unless you charge for them. Counsellors automatically charge a full fee for a short notice cancellation. Only you can decide whether it is better to risk losing the goodwill of the client or cope with the loss of your income.

In practice, however, you will probably need to be flexible. If someone has crashed their car on the way to you, or a relative has died suddenly, you may be prepared to waive your cancellation fee. But if clients forget, you may want to charge them. Sometimes they will offer to pay anyway, as then they no longer feel under an obligation to you. Some therapists charge a proportion of their fee for cancellations with less than 48 hours and a full fee for less than 24 hours. Others charge a full fee regardless. Occasionally you may lose a client because you charged them a cancellation fee, but that is their loss – a more reliable client usually appears in their place.

TERMS AND CONDITIONS

If you don't already have a set of terms and conditions, you should think about writing yourself one. There is more information about terms and conditions in Chapter 2.

As already mentioned, you might want to exercise your discretion from time to time in situations where it is clear that the client has a genuine reason for late cancellation and/or the circumstances behind their cancellation were out of their reasonable control. It's entirely up to you – but it's better to set out the default situation and then choose to be lenient on occasion rather than to have no policy at all and be effectively at the mercy of your clients' whims. It is easier to waive a cancellation fee than to ask for one from a client who does not expect it.

It is worth having a similar clause to deal with latecomers. I believe that your other clients who are on time should not be put out by those who are less punctual. From the client's point of view it is infuriating to rush to an appointment to be kept waiting because someone else was late. If you have time to accommodate someone who is late through no fault of their own, you may choose to do so. But don't put your whole day out because of a client who is habitually late; you'll soon get to know who they are.

It is also worth printing your terms and conditions (or an abbreviated form of them) on your brochure, and displaying them on your website (if you have one). If you display them on your website, make sure they are not buried on an obscure page which no one will ever find! Transparency is what you're aiming for – you're trying to make your relationship with your clients easier, not more difficult.

TURNING AWAY A CLIENT

It is worth pointing out that we do not have to treat everyone who asks us for a treatment. Just as a publican can refuse to serve someone in his or her pub, we can choose whom we wish to treat. What do you do if you form a violent aversion to someone who comes to you for treatment? What if they drain you? The answer depends on whether or not you can put your feelings on one side and give them a good treatment while retaining your integrity and your sanity. I don't believe it is necessary to like all those that I treat, but it is vital to respect and tolerate them. I have one or two who have the effect of making my heart sink when I see their names in the diary. However, they must feel they get a reasonable treatment or they would not come back for more.

It is very empowering to turn someone away occasionally. I once treated a lady with Multiple Sclerosis. She parked her car inconveniently for my neighbours (couldn't park well because of the MS). Then she demanded a drastically reduced fee (had no money because of the MS) and wanted an extra long treatment (because of the MS). It had to be the same time each week (poor memory due to MS). She made offensive personal comments about my house (uninhibited because of MS). I finally managed to usher her out after 2 hours while she complained that I hadn't shown her any photos of my children. After she had gone I felt as if I had to brush bits of her off me. I dreaded her return, and wrote to her suggesting she find someone else.

If you do turn someone away try to do it as gently as possible, but not so gently that they don't get the message! You could say that you believe you are not the right therapist for them or that they "need a fresh pair of hands". In this way you present getting rid of them as having their best interests at heart. Again, you might want to put something in your terms and conditions to this effect – that is, that you reserve the right to turn away a client at your discretion.

AVAILABILITY

It is nine o'clock on Friday evening and you are pleasantly relaxed after a couple of drinks. The phone rings – a potential new client is enquiring about an appointment. Do you answer the phone? Is your speech slurred? Do you sound coherent and can you sell yourself well? Will they be put off by the fact that you have been drinking (conveniently forgetting that they rang at an intrusive time)?

It may be an automatic reaction to answer the phone, but your answering machine is your best ally on these occasions. I have had whole weeks when I would not have had an uninterrupted meal without the answering machine. I have also been phoned at 6am (a farmer), at 11.30pm (sorry, I forgot to come this evening), in the middle of a dinner party (to change an appointment the following week), at 8.30am on New Year's day, and on many other bank holidays.

If you wish to reduce this kind of intrusion, it is worth telling your clients a good time to get hold of you. I deliberately do not return calls which I consider intrusive until the next day. You might consider leaving a time when you can be contacted on your answering phone message.

One of the disadvantages of being self employed is that it is difficult to get away from your work. Make sure you take regular holidays or short breaks. It is tempting to be too available when you first start out. You will become tired and stale if you don't ensure that you recharge your batteries regularly. If that happens, your reputation as a good therapist will suffer.

COMPLAINTS ABOUT COLLEAGUES

When working as a therapist, you may well hear stories or allegations about other therapists. It is possible that these are merely malicious but I have to say that whenever I have heard such things they have turned out to be true. I had to think carefully about what to do when several of my female clients, who did not know each other, revealed that they had been inappropriately touched by a male colleague. People often believe that they are the only one this has happened to, so it is important to let them know that this may not be the case without saying outright that you have heard the allegation before. You should acknowledge what they say without criticising your colleague.

On another occasion, someone phoned me in a highly distressed state and described a serious indecent assault by a colleague of mine. I contacted the police, who investigated the allegation and discovered that he had done the same to a large number of women. He was eventually tried, found guilty and placed on the sex offenders' register. Sadly, all those years ago, there was no mechanism to prevent him setting up a new practice elsewhere. The current move to regulate complementary therapy will hopefully allow some redress to such victims in the future.

COMPLAINTS FROM CLIENTS

Unfortunately, complaints are part of professional life- you are extremely lucky if you never have one. However, you need to know how to deal with one should the situation arise. It is always distressing to be told that your treatment has done harm rather than good, but it is important to remain calm.

The first approach is likely to be a verbal complaint. It is possible to acknowledge the person's distress *without admitting liability*. It is better to say "I'm sorry to hear that", rather than a defensive "Well, it's not *my* fault."

If you have written comprehensive notes on each treatment, you will be able to refer back to how the client was feeling and what you did on that occasion. Try to find out what the person did and how they felt after the treatment. Did they follow your advice, such as to rest or drink plenty of water? What else might provoke the symptoms they are experiencing? You may well find on closer questioning that they are trying to blame you when they have behaved unwisely after a treatment.

I remember one client phoning to say that after a massage from me she had had to see her osteopath several times and to spend a week in bed. When I looked back over my notes I had recorded that I had given her 17 treatments previously, from which she had suffered no adverse effects. The first thing I had written about her that day was 'complaining of feeling generally achy'. I had also noted that I advised her to rest after our session. On further questioning, I discovered that she had played in a tennis tournament immediately after the session, despite my telling her that this was not advisable for a 65-year-old woman with a chronic back problem. I told her that I thought she had been unwise to ignore my advice, and reminded her that she complained of general aches and pains before I had even touched her. She did not pursue the complaint.

GENERAL GUIDELINES ON DEALING WITH COMPLAINTS

- do not respond defensively – listen and acknowledge *without* accepting liability
- remain calm – you are trying to defuse a situation *before* it blows up into a complaint
- try not to take it personally
- do not offer refunds or mention your insurance cover
- try to find out if something other than your treatment could have caused the problem
- talk it over with a colleague or your training school if you wish

- refer back to your notes to see if there is any hint of a pre-existing problem
- make notes of what is said during telephone calls
- if you think the client will make a formal claim against you, contact your insurer without delay

CHECKLIST

- ❏ is your First Aid certificate (and First Aid kit) up to date?
- ❏ is your phone answering message professional and unambiguous?
- ❏ have you formulated a way of turning away a client?
- ❏ have you decided on your cancellation policy?
- ❏ what will you do about latecomers?
- ❏ have you decided on the hours you will be available?
- ❏ are you confident about dealing with nuisance phone calls?
- ❏ are you prepared for dealing with a complaint if one arises?

8 LOOKING AFTER YOURSELF

Being is born of not being.   THE TAO TE CHING BY LAO TSU

You will only be able to sell yourself and your therapy and give treatments which benefit your clients if you feel well and full of energy and enthusiasm. It is essential that you look after your workforce – yourself! There are a number of ways of doing this.

Firstly, you should set your working times *and keep to them*. This will help protect your energy levels. If you make yourself too available, you will quickly become tired and stale. It is amazing how clients suddenly find they can come at a time more convenient to you, when they realise you are not free otherwise! It is also important to take regular breaks or holidays. Therapy can be a very draining occupation and you will need to have fun and recharge your batteries: your clients can only benefit from it.

I personally have gained enormously from the support of other therapists. We all help one another to maintain our health, as well as providing vital listening and friendship. This reduces any possible sense of isolation and also creates the opportunity for referrals both to them and to you. (This is an excellent, low cost way of increasing your business.) My colleagues have supported me as I have supported them, through some very tough times, with treatments, emails and phone calls.

When my father died many years ago, a colleague told me that I should be kind to myself at least once a day. She meant soak in a bath, read a book, go for a walk, phone or meet a friend. I followed her advice and it helped so much I think we should all do that every day!

One of the great things about complementary therapy is that

your clients are enabled to learn to look after themselves and take responsibility for their health. It goes without saying that if you advocate your therapy, healthy eating, exercise and fun for others, you should practise what you preach and do the same yourself.

DEALING WITH 'STUFF'

Most of us have experienced occasions when a friend comes round for a good moan. They feel marvellous afterwards and we are left with the crud they have dumped on us. This situation is magnified when we treat clients, particularly in massage where we have skin-to-skin contact.

It is generally accepted that we hold anger, distress and other emotions in our muscles. Our clients are therefore highly likely to release these feelings during treatment. What do we do if we feel we are left with it, or something presses our own emotional buttons? I once heard a doctor describe it as 'emotional cross-infection'. Do we also risk cross-infecting our other clients emotionally if we do not take steps to deal with it?

- use a psychic protection ritual before touching anybody
- wear designated clothes for work
- use clean towels and paper couch roll for each person (if you need them in your therapy)
- open the window for fresh air between clients
- wash your hands in cold water between clients
- cleanse the room with incense/candles/crystals/flower essences/smudge stick
- take Bach Flower Rescue Remedy
- if you suspect someone will upset you, take a few drops of Bach Flower Walnut remedy in water before seeing them

- shower and change your clothes after you have finished work.

Psychic protection

It is difficult to talk about psychic protection without sounding mysterious or airy-fairy. However, it is such an important aspect of therapeutic work that I mention it here and leave you to formulate your own personal protection. Most of the successful therapists I know have some form of protection ritual, and a way of cleansing themselves afterwards. It does not matter whether this is hugging trees, using crystals, or soaking in the bath. The important thing is that it works for you.

Much depends on your beliefs and sensitivities. The simplest protection is to imagine yourself enveloped in a huge ball of white light through which nothing negative can penetrate. Judy Hall, in her book, *The Art of Psychic Protection*, suggests stepping into a hoop of light which you can pull up around you. She also has some wonderful images of psychic laser guns and vacuum cleaners to remove any lingering 'nasties'.

I had one client, later diagnosed as schizophrenic, who was very difficult and disturbed. I used to visualise myself in a diving bell so that I could treat him without problems. I also visualise the spider plant in my treatment room soaking up any negativity.

If I feel that my treatment room is harbouring anything negative, I mentally sweep the room, open the window wide and allow the negativity to fall into the earth where it becomes neutralised. You can also 'smudge' a room with a sage wand. Light the end, blow on it to get it well alight, then waft the smoke around the room, paying particular attention to the corners. Hold a bowl underneath as bits of burning sage may drop off the wand. You can clean your aura with it in the same way. When you have finished, stub the wand out in a bowl of sand.

Your own stuff

Occasionally when someone confides in me I am left feeling distressed by it. Showering and changing my clothes is a useful ritual for shedding the day's distress. If that fails, I take Rescue Remedy, or Star of Bethlehem. I always burn an incense stick at the end of every day as part of my ritual. (It is good for getting rid of cooking smells, too). Remember that colleagues can be supportive when you need them. Sometimes all you need is a treatment to re-charge your batteries, or a friendly understanding ear.

Give yourself a time limit for dealing with distress. If you are no better by your self-imposed deadline, seek professional help. If you have done a good job of making contacts you will know a psychotherapist or counsellor who will be able to help. If you think I am exaggerating the need for psychic protection and dealing with stuff, here is a list of some of the things I have had divulged to me:

- rape (at least two, including that of a 9-year-old)
- sexual abuse (four or five)
- violent relationship (several)
- indecent assault by another therapist (several)
- death of client's child/ren (several)
- client sent to prison (he stated he was innocent)
- suicide of client's son
- messy divorce
- severe psychiatric illness and/or depression
- post-traumatic stress disorder
- injured in and survived a plane crash

If several of these crop up in a short space of time, you can end up feeling pretty chewed up. In order to remain effective as a therapist and human being, you need to find ways of coping with and processing your distress. Counsellors are obliged to have regular supervision in order to work well. As there is no obligation on you to do that, I suggest you find your own appropriate form of support and care, preferably *before* you need it.

This helps *you* to cope, but what about the poor client? Most of us are not trained counsellors and do not have the necessary skills to deal with such traumas. It is important that we acknowledge their distress while making it clear that we cannot help. I say something like "I can see this is very distressing for you. Have you thought of who you might go and talk to about it?" I then suggest a referral to a colleague who has the skills to help them.

I leave this subject with a quote.

"Caring persons must be prepared to suffer within the suffering of others. We shall only be able to do this when we have enough health within ourselves to be able to continually expose ourselves to the person in need of care. As we search for a deeper and greater awareness of our own emotional and spiritual needs, I would suggest that only in our growing awareness of these needs, dare we enter into the sufferings of others. Dare we ask the other person the real reason for his suffering? Dare we ask what this suffering is doing and/or means? Dare we communicate in such a manner as to enable him and ourselves to grow through his suffering, our mutual suffering? Caring persons are not healers, at best they are *enablers of healing*" (my italics).

Kirkpatrick, (*Nursing Times*, 1980)

Support groups

Complementary therapy support groups have a number of things to offer the newly qualified therapist:

- they help you to meet other therapists
- other therapists get to know you
- they provide the stimulation of new ideas and professional development
- they offer support which helps reduce isolation
- they sometimes print lists of therapists, helping to generate work
- they can provide the opportunity to make friends/ swap treatments
- they help keep you up to date with developments in your therapy

What do you do if there is no support group in your area? Start one! If you don't feel up to organising a big group you could get together with a few therapists. If your home is not suitable, you could meet at a pub or village hall. When I first embarked on setting up a support group I was surprised and delighted by the friendly, positive response I received from other therapists.

The group I started grew to about 30 therapists who met 4 times a year. Some of the group have become really close friends and I value them greatly. We had a mixture of meetings with speakers, and social occasions. Therapists also swap skills. For example, one person with computer skills does a job in exchange for some essential oils. Therapists new to the area can find out about work possibilities and feel less isolated. We produced a list of therapists which we distributed to health food shops, leisure centres, dentists, libraries, and anywhere else we could. The initial work of setting it up was well worth the effort.

PROFESSIONAL ORGANISATIONS

At the end of this book there is a list of some professional organisations. (There are more listed on my website www.successfultherapist.co.uk). There are many benefits of belonging to one (or more if you choose):

- your clients will see you as a responsible professional person adhering to high standards
- your organisation may well have representation on one of the major regulatory bodies
- they provide support and guidance for members
- they may have local support groups where you can meet other therapists
- they may provide workshops or seminars and CPD
- they usually have some powers of regulating members who do not adhere to their code of conduct
- they provide contacts in what can be an isolated profession
- some provide a helpline
- most offer insurance
- most list therapists online which can bring you new clients
- they may sell related products
- they produce a magazine

CONTINUING PROFESSIONAL DEVELOPMENT

It is essential that you keep up to date in your therapy and gain stimulation from new ideas. Most professional organisations now insist on a number of CPD hours per year and require evidence that it has been completed. It is usual for this time to be spent in different ways such as research, reading, attending courses lectures and workshops, exhibitions and conferences. Further training need not necessarily mean lengthy expensive courses. It is possible to find one-day workshops or evening lectures to interest you. Some support groups put on excellent talks by knowledgeable speakers. While you are less busy, use your time to read around your subject and consolidate your knowledge. Once you become busy there may not be enough time for this. You should also consider subscribing to a relevant journal. Occasional visits to health exhibitions can be useful: your training school may be glad of your help if they are taking part. They may also give study days, conferences and workshops which will contribute to your CPD hours. Attending these can also help reduce any sense of isolation you may feel. Tracking your CPD is satisfying as it provides evidence that your practice and abilities are growing and developing.

SELF REFLECTION

The comedian Billy Connolly once said, "Wisdom is the constant questioning of where you are. And when you stop wanting to know, you're dead." It is important to reflect on your practice, tracking your progress, what works and what doesn't. This doesn't mean being unnecessarily hard on yourself. It means being self critical in a constructive way. If you feel you made a mistake or took the wrong approach with someone, don't beat yourself up, but learn from it and move on. (And apologise if that is necessary.)

It is also important to know when you need help to develop your practice. This could be with a life coach, a counsellor, further training, a mentor, a small business advisor or simply by further reading around your subject.

CHECKLIST

☐ have you organised your work schedule to maximise your free time?

☐ have you booked some holiday in your diary?

☐ do you try to eat rest and sleep well?

☐ do you have fun regularly?

☐ have you formulated a psychic protection ritual?

☐ have you made contact with other therapists for mutual support?

☐ do you know someone you can talk to if something upsets you?

☐ have you researched a support group?

☐ have you joined a professional organisation?

☐ do you know your CPD requirement and have you planned to do some?

☐ do you reflect on your practice and self criticise constructively?

9 Managing your money

*Learning to charge properly is a vital key to abundance. Affirm
that you will never devalue yourself by charging less than what
you feel you are worth.*

Stuart Wilde, The Trick to Money is Having Some

Your attitude to money

Do you believe that because you are caring for people it somehow
isn't right for you to take their money? It is amazing how many
therapists have problems reconciling helping others and earning
a living. Yet even the best healers need to eat and pay their bills.
Are you clear that you are offering something of value, and therefore
you deserve to be paid accordingly? Professional people charge
professional fees in return for a professional service. Your clients
have the choice of paying what you ask and expecting a high
standard of care from you or of doing without. If someone is
thinking of coming to you for a treatment, they expect you to be
fully trained, competent, insured, and up to date on the latest
techniques and best practice. It will have cost you a considerable
amount of time, hard work and money to achieve this: it is perfectly
reasonable for you to expect appropriate remuneration in return.
A colleague of mine makes a point of charging above the going
rate. He is always fully booked because people believe that as he
charges more, he must be the best!

Calculating and setting fees

I receive more requests for advice on this than anything else, so it
obviously causes a few headaches. If you pitch your fees very low
you are undervaluing your therapy and yourself. You will upset

your colleagues who charge a more realistic rate, and potential clients may be suspicious of someone who charges so little. You might decide to charge a low fee when you first start, as a way of attracting clients. If so, make it clear that this is for a limited period only and what your full fee will be when the special rate comes to an end. Otherwise clients may be shocked when your fees rise dramatically. You should review your fees annually. You may choose not to increase them each year but you should make a conscious decision about it.

If potential clients think they can find equally good treatment more cheaply elsewhere, let them. I once treated someone who thought my fees were high, as she could have massage elsewhere much more cheaply. She phoned me later to say that the cheaper massage was nowhere near as good as mine, so she would prefer to come to me in future, even if she couldn't afford to come as often. In therapy, the lowest price is not necessarily the best treatment; you can easily be the cheapest but you cannot also be the best. Think about your motivation. There are times when all of us feel tired and disheartened, and occasionally only the thought of earning the money keeps us going. How motivated will you be if what you are earning barely covers your costs?

Start by investigating the range of fees charged by other therapists in your area. Make a few phone calls, ask them what they charge and get an idea of the time, type, level and professionalism of the service they are providing for that fee. When you have done this background research ask yourself where in that range you wish to position the value of your own work. Be realistic and don't expect to be at the top of the range until you are more experienced.

This will give you a price which you can charge, but it is also worth calculating how much it costs you to give each treatment, in order to assess the profit you will make from it. There is no point in charging say, £20 for a treatment if it costs you £21 to give it. There is more about this later.

FREE TREATMENTS

When starting out it is a good idea to offer some free treatments. However, you should think about how many and for how long you will do this. When I was setting out as a therapist, I gave a friend a free treatment. She immediately told her neighbour, a hospital consultant, who became a regular client herself and who also recommended me to her patients. The free treatment helped establish my practice.

Make sure however, that people do not take advantage of you. Another person I treated for nothing kept telling me it was a shame I couldn't have massage as often as her. If she had paid me, I could have done!

REDUCING FEES

You will undoubtedly be asked from time to time to reduce your fees for someone. The important issue here, as with free treatments, is that you are comfortable with the arrangement and do not feel taken for granted. It is perfectly acceptable to say no. Remember too, that you will only be able to reduce your fees for the minority if you charge a full fee to the majority. Deciding who that minority should be is the difficult part!

Some years ago I went to massage a man in his own home. Having gained admission at the electronic gates, a servant took my couch upstairs, past an enormous swimming pool, into the gymnasium. I was amazed when he asked me to reduce my fees, but he accepted with good grace when I refused. However, he managed to get the better of me when I went back another time. He insisted on paying me in cash but he didn't have quite enough on him. He promised to pay me next time, but never contacted me again. (I later learned that he owned several extremely smart hotels in central London.)

A colleague reduced her fees after hearing a sob story. One day she happened to drive past the client's house. When she saw the expensive cars, the stable block and swimming pool, resentment set in.

You will have to judge each case on its individual merits, but do beware of taking on other peoples' poverty. I have been given some amazing reasons for asking for a reduction including going on safari, going on holiday, going to the theatre, just bought a new car, just bought a second home, three horses to feed, and paying for children at private school.

Whether or not you reduce your fees depends on how much you want to see a particular client. If you do decide to reduce fees you have several options:

- reduce for a short time agreed by you and the client
- reduce for a client who introduces another client
- offer a 'standby' rate for a short notice appointment
- reduce long-term treatment fees by a small amount

RELUCTANT PAYERS

In my experience, if people value what you do for them, they will pay you, as they will want to see you again. However, occasionally it is necessary to chase a client for payment. It is useful to have a computer for typing and keeping a record of your bills. In 20 years of practice I have had only two bounced cheques, one of which cleared when re-presented. I had to write off the other one as the client had also given me a false address. I have written off a few cancellations, but this is more commonly an area of negotiation between the therapist and client. It is easier to take payment at the end of the consultation than to send out a bill. If a potentially awkward situation develops, address it quickly before it gets out of hand.

SPECIAL OFFERS AND DISCOUNTS

Some therapies, for example beauty therapy, lend themselves better to this form of marketing than others. You could offer a discount for a specified period of time, or reward your regular clientele with appropriate reductions such as if they introduce a friend.

MEANS OF PAYMENT

You will need to decide how you wish to accept payment from your clients. Will you choose cash, cheques, BACS, credit and/or debit cards or all of those? If you are prepared to accept payment by credit or debit card you will have to pay for the equipment to read the card and a fee for each transaction to the credit card company.

For therapists working on their own and for individual clients the simplest method is probably cash or cheque. If you work for a company, they may well pay direct into your bank account. If you work within a practice, the cost of credit card equipment is usually met by the practice owner.

MAKING A PROFIT

So far we have looked at the amount of money you receive. However, it is just as important to keep track of the amount of money you spend. There are many different types of costs which you will incur depending on the type of therapy you provide and how you go about setting up your business. These include (in accountant speak!):

Capital expenditure (typically infrequent or one off payments to buy an item of equipment) for example:

- couches
- desks and chairs
- computer equipment
- filing/record cabinets
- telephone

Fixed costs (which if you are in business, you pay whether you earn or not) will be items such as:

- insurance
- rent under a lease
- professional membership fees
- business rates on premises
- Continuing Professional Development
- annual advertising
- telephone rental charges
- account books and professional fees

Although you can choose whether to incur some of the expenditure, once the decision has been taken (e.g. an advertisement in the phone book) it does not matter whether you see one client or 100, the cost will be the same. However, the period over which the costs are fixed will vary. For example, your insurance premium will typically be fixed for a year, whereas your telephone rental charge is normally for three months.

Variable costs are dependent on how many clients you see. For example:

- travel costs
- oils and paper towels
- consulting room hire/fees paid to a clinic

- laundry costs
- appointment cards
- supervision
- credit/debit card or cheque processing fees

If your income from each client does not cover your variable costs it is simply not worth working! You will spend more money than you earn for each person you treat. Similarly, if you don't cover your variable and fixed costs over the period in which the costs are fixed, you are losing money and have nothing left for all your efforts. In the longer term you may have to replace your capital equipment, so you also need to make enough profit to cover this cost as well.

Having decided what your fees are going to be, it is worthwhile checking how many clients you have to treat before you start making money. Let's take a simple example:

David is a therapist who works from a clinic but has to provide his own equipment. He is considering a range of fees of between £20 and £50 per hour. He has calculated his costs to be:

Couch cost £1,250 which he plans to replace after five years

Professional indemnity insurance	£150
Professional subscriptions	£100
Annual training courses	£250
Advertisement in phone book	£100
Room hire from the clinic	£11 per hour
Paper towels/wipes	£1 per client
Travel cost to the client	£2
Free bottle of water supplied to each client	£1

If we plot these costs on a graph (below) we can see that the cost per client falls rapidly to start with as David's fixed costs are spread over the number of clients but then begin to level off. However, he has to earn at least £15 per client in order to cover his variable costs of room hire, towels, travelling and his decision to give every client a free bottle of water.

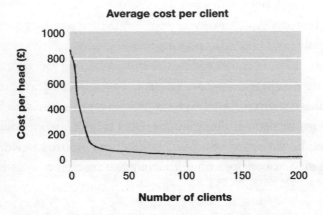

Average cost per client

You can also look at how many clients you have to treat before you cover all of your fixed costs and so start to make a real profit. This is known as the breakeven point. It will depend on the level of fees you decided to charge (as discussed earlier in this chapter) and the period over which the costs are fixed. In David's case the fixed costs broadly cover one year.

The chart opposite shows the level of income which David will earn depending on the amount at which he sets his fees. Compare this with the amounts which he will spend and you can see that at £20 per hour he will have to treat 170 people per year to break even. However, if he can charge £50 an hour he will be making a profit after just 25 treatments. Further details are set out in Appendix 1.

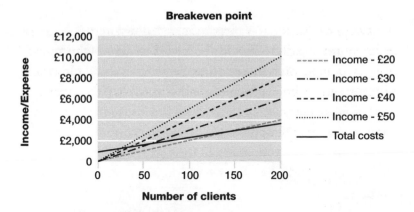

Breakeven point

FLUCTUATIONS IN INCOME

Unfortunately, if you are self employed, you are likely to suffer fluctuations in income. This may arise because of market forces, such as recession, when you take a holiday, or if you are unwell and so unable to work for a time. You may also experience a patch of cancellations. These are the most difficult to deal with – if clients have given you sufficient notice you can't really charge them, but on the other hand you were expecting to earn the money and may not fill the gap. I sometimes find myself resenting my clients, most of whom are in paid employment and have no idea of how their change of plans has affected me. I try to let my clients know, without making them feel so guilty that they don't come back.

Some therapists like to have another part-time job. Even if it doesn't pay much, it can make a big difference by providing a regular income. This helps relieve anxiety about the reduction in income in quiet times, while paying some bills. It may also give you some respite from the exhausting business of 'giving out' to clients. It is worth putting aside some money in busier times to help when things are quiet. Try to have around three months' income saved for a rainy day. If you have prepared a cash flow forecast as part of your business plan, you should also have some idea of the months in which you are likely to have particularly high expenditure or low income, such as holiday periods (either yours or your clients').

If you are planning to move from full-time employment to complementary therapy, you could ask your current employer to allow you to reduce your hours. In this way you can begin to build your practice gradually while having the security of some regular income.

Another option is to practise more than one therapy as this increases your potential client base. If you do this, be careful not to offer so many that potential clients are put off by a long list of things they may not have heard of. Teaching, adult education classes and running workshops can increase your income too.

A recession affects everyone but having a loyal band of regular clients may help to minimise the effects of it. Even if clients are unable to afford to visit you for a while, they are likely to want to come back as soon as they can, and will continue to recommend you to their friends. You could consider 'beat the recession' special offers for a short time: if you are paying rent on somewhere to work this should at least cover your costs.

A recession provides the opportunity to be creative and think up different ways of earning a living. I heard of a pub which hires a hairdresser one evening a week. While waiting for a haircut, clients buy a drink and chat with their friends. The pub landlord is happy because it brings in new customers and the hairdresser gains new clients. Perhaps you can think of somewhere where there could be a captive audience and ask if you could offer mini treatments. If the clients aren't coming to you, you need to find a way to reach them.

It is often small businesses which flourish during hard times, because they have the ability to adapt more quickly than their larger rivals. A small motor boat can change direction quickly and easily. A large cruise ship needs instruction from the captain, those instructions to be carried out by a number of others, then the ship itself takes a long time to make the manoeuvre. Remember that you, as a small motor boat, have the advantage of speed and adaptability.

CHECKLIST

- ❑ are you clear that you are offering something of value?
- ❑ have you decided what your fees will be?
- ❑ have you decided your policy on reducing fees?
- ❑ have you chosen the ways in which you will accept payment?
- ❑ what is the going rate locally?
- ❑ will you offer a reduced rate when you first start?
- ❑ if so, for how long before raising your fees?
- ❑ can you motivate yourself to give a good treatment if you reduce your rate?
- ❑ are you prepared to give any free treatments?
- ❑ what do you consider to be your value (in terms of what you offer in a treatment)?
- ❑ what outgoings will you have to cover?
- ❑ are you saving money to cover your bills including tax?

10 PLANNING FOR BUSINESS SUCCESS

Business must be run at a profit, else it will die. But if you run a business solely for profit, then also it must die, for it no longer has a reason to live.   HENRY FORD.

It is all too easy, particularly when starting out, to pay insufficient attention to the business side of what you do. When you did your training, you practised on case studies, and from there, you probably started trying to earn a bit of extra income by treating family, friends, and friends of friends. At that stage, business probably didn't seem to come into it.

But if you're serious about making a proper living from complementary therapy, you need to start running your practice like a business rather than as a hobby or handy sideline. Too many therapists give up after a year or two, regardless of how good they are, just because they haven't got to grips with this single principle.

Put simply, the more clued up you are about your business, the more successful you are likely to be – and the more successful you are, the longer you will be able to continue doing what you love!

GET WRITING

Take some time to write a business plan, even if it is for your eyes only. Research consistently shows that those who don't plan, plan to fail, and those who put their plans down on paper are much more likely to succeed than those who don't.

So get writing – whether you're just starting out, or already in business, make sure you plan. It's never too late. Write down what you want to be doing in a year, three years, and five years from now, and work out what you need to do to achieve those goals. Writing it down will help you focus on what you really want to do and how you're going to do it.

CREATING A WINNING BUSINESS PLAN

Despite what you might think or have been told, there's no set structure to a business plan. The key is simply to present a snapshot of where you are now, where you want to be in x years' time, and what you need to do to get to that point.

For your plan to be worthwhile, it should be comprehensible to those who don't necessarily know you or your business very well, but who might be able to assist you along the way – such as your bank manager, your accountant, a possible investor, or a marketing advisor.

Your business plan should show at a glance what shape your business is in at present, where it could most use some help, and what the possible risks are. For this reason, you should be as specific as possible, particularly when it comes to the financial side of things.

Your cash flow forecast is vital here. Don't just guess at this stage – sit down with a calculator and carefully work out your potential income. Make sure that you include all your expenditure, too – for example, your room rent, phone rental, travel costs, insurance, the cost of couch roll, oils, and so forth.

Make a start by creating an Excel spreadsheet (or similar) for the next 12 months. Then have a section for income, and a section for expenditure. In each section, you'll need to have 2 columns – one for your forecast, and one for the actual expenditure/income.

Your forecast will initially involve a bit of guesswork, based on what you think you can reasonably achieve in the month. You'll already have an idea of what things cost from your training. You'll probably also have decided what you want to charge for your treatments. Now all you have to do is estimate roughly how many sales you'll make in a month.

If you're just starting out, you might want to set your income forecast on the low side for the first 2 or 3 months to take into account the fact that it will take a while to become established. You can then increase it little by little over the rest of the year. Especially where your income is concerned, if you set your initial forecast figure low, you'll give yourself a good chance of being able to insert a higher figure in your 'Actual' column – which can be a great morale booster in the early stages of building your business! But don't be silly about it – aim for as near-realistic figures as you can.

So, for example, for your first 3 months, your chart might look something like the example opposite.

The more detailed your financial projections are, the better you will understand your business, and the more in control of it you'll feel. And the more often you run your spreadsheet, the more accurate you'll become at forecasting your cash flow.

And not only will your business be less likely to fail, but it could be up to *50% more profitable* than if you didn't have a plan, according to research. Now, isn't that an incentive to get planning?

Template business plan

1. Summary
- an introduction to you and your (proposed) business/product/service, and why your business will succeed!
- financial overview (existing capital, first-year profit projections, any funding requirements)

	Month 1		Month 2		Month 3	
	Forecast	Actual	Forecast	Actual	Forecast	Actual
Income						
Product sales						
Massages						
Bank loan+						
TOTAL	£0.00	£0.00	£0.00	£0.00	£0.00	£0.00
Expenditure						
Rent						
Rates						
Gas, elec						
Telephone						
Insurance						
Advertising						
Printing						
Postage						
Towels						
Oils						
Couch roll						
Loan repayment						
Drawings*						
TOTAL	£0.00	£0.00	£0.00	£0.00	£0.00	£0.00
Income–expenditure	£0.00	£0.00	£0.00	£0.00	£0.00	£0.00
Bank opening balance	£0.00	£0.00	£0.00	£0.00	£0.00	£0.00
Bank closing balance	£0.00	£0.00	£0.00	£0.00	£0.00	£0.00

+ If you have a bank loan, enter the monthly amount you receive here. Obviously, in this particular case, your forecast amount is very likely to be the same as your actual amount!

* Drawings = money you pay yourself or others.

2. Management

- details of your business experience
- why the business has been started

3. Product/Service

- details of your main products and/or services

4. Marketing

- your past, present, and future sales capability
- your main competitors (and their strengths and weaknesses)
- your expected customer profile
- summary of where you fit in – why there's room for you in the market

5. Sales

- your product/service's Unique Selling Proposition – or, what makes you special!
- your prices and/or pricing policy
- advertising and planned promotions (e.g. website development, mailshots, exhibitions, etc)

6. Operational

- business location
- existing equipment (including transport), and costs to date
- proposed equipment

7. Short-term trading

- short-term objectives (e.g. level of sales you want to achieve for the next 12-month period)
- contingency plans (think about what risks might threaten your business and prevent you from reaching your targets – what are they? How will you deal with them? For example, what would happen if you became seriously ill for a few weeks? What would you do if you didn't make any sales for a couple of months?)

8. Financial

- Profit and loss account   )
- Balance sheet   ) projected for
- Monthly cash flow forecast)   the next 2–3 years

If you're working on your own as a sole trader, then you probably don't need to worry too much about the second document. But whatever you do, don't forget that all-important cash flow forecast and accompanying profit and loss account!

11 ACCOUNTS AND TAXATION

It is better to have a permanent income than be fascinating

OSCAR WILDE

DECIDE THE TYPE OF LEGAL STRUCTURE FOR YOUR BUSINESS

When you start out in business as a complementary therapist you may be:

- an employee (for example working for someone else at a spa)
- self employed (where you work for yourself either from home or at other locations)
- in partnership (working together with a colleague) or
- you could set up your own company

An employee will work a set number of hours in a room provided by their employer, be provided with the equipment they need for their job and receive a regular income including holiday and possibly sickness pay. Theirs is the most straightforward position. Their income is assured for as long as they remain employed. They don't need to keep business accounts and their employer should deduct income tax (Pay As You Earn) and National Insurance from their weekly or monthly income. If they have no other sources of income they will not normally have to complete a Tax Return.

Many complementary therapists work on a self-employed basis where they are in business on their own account. They are ultimately responsible for how the business is run, and are in control of what they do, and when, how and where they provide treatment. They will provide the equipment necessary to do their work and will be personally responsible if anything should go wrong. Their income may fluctuate but they will receive the benefits from the growth of their business over time. Self employed people will have to keep detailed accounts of their income, expenditure and assets. They must complete a Tax Return each year which they send to Her Majesty's Revenue and Customs (HMRC). There is more information on the HMRC website at www.hmrc.gov.uk.

A few therapists may start their practice in partnership with a friend or colleague. Others may join together once their practices have started. You will need legal advice before the partnership begins, to establish the basis under which the partners will act. It follows that it is vital to choose the right partner from the outset. The partnership will be required to keep detailed accounts and each partner will have to report their share of the profits on their Tax Return.

Self-employed people or those working in partnership will have unlimited liability for any costs which arise in the business. If the business makes a loss, it will have to be covered out of their other income or personal assets such as their own home. You may therefore wish to consider setting up your own company where you are the sole shareholder. A company's liability for losses is normally limited to the amount of money you put into it as share capital. It provides some financial protection. However, it also involves additional administration and costs. For example, you will have to:

- prepare accounts each year and file these at Companies House for which a fee is payable
- treat yourself as an employee and account for PAYE and National Insurance on any salary you take from the company

- complete a Tax Return for the company and
  for yourself.

For most therapists with good liability insurance, the costs and hassle of setting up and running their own company are likely to outweigh the benefits.

KEEPING RECORDS

Whether you are self employed or in partnership you must keep detailed accounts and supporting records. The key documents which you should keep are:

- a book in which to record all business income and expenditure
- receipts for any business expenditure incurred
- a copy of any invoices issued
- bank statements
- cheque book stubs
- paying in slips
- appointments diary

You should keep these records for at least six years after the end of the tax year, preferably longer.

Accountants will usually ask you to use an analysis book in which you write all the receipts on the left-hand side and all the expenses on the right. For each item of income, identify the client who paid you and the date. If you issue an invoice, keep a copy and record the invoice number as a reference point in your analysis book so that you can find a copy if required. It is best to just use the client's surname so that they cannot be identified by your accountant or anyone else looking at your books (such as HMRC). This is to preserve your client's privacy. If a client has an unusual surname which might lead to their being identified, or they are in the public eye, I use a code name to avoid any risk of embarrassment.

For each item of expenditure, record in your analysis book to whom you made the payment and what it was for, so that you can show that it was a business expense. If you like using computers there are many software packages around that will help you do the job. I use a simple Excel spreadsheet. Appendix 2 is an example. Whatever system you use you will still need to find some time each week, if not each day, to keep your accounts up to date.

The kind of things you should record as a business expense are:

- stationery, business cards, brochures, postage
- books and subscriptions to professional journals
- insurance costs
- room hire
- special clothing – tunics, gowns or overalls
- further training and associated costs like travel, parking, meals away from home
- secretarial assistance
- telephone call costs and standing charges for a business line
- accountancy and other professional fees
- advertising
- staff costs for any people that you employ
- bank charges and interest associated with a business loan
- any equipment such as a couch, covers, towels and oils
- computers and relevant software

Each payment should be entered in the analysis book separately with a reference to identify the invoice which is being paid. This will help you to check which bills have been paid and to find the invoice again if you need to. I use a simple reference of the year of the expense followed by a sequential number which I have written on to the invoice. If you don't have an invoice, perhaps because it is a direct debit, you should still have something which explains why you are paying that amount, e.g. an annual insurance policy which you are paying in instalments.

If you issue invoices to your clients you should give each one its own unique number and keep a copy on an invoice file. Although you have to issue an invoice if you are registered for VAT, you don't necessarily have to do so otherwise. Where therapies are provided directly to the person paying for them, they will usually pay your fee at the time of their visit. They will not need an invoice, unless they are claiming the money back from someone else – perhaps under a medical insurance policy. However, if you are providing treatments to a number of people but being paid by someone else (for example, an insurance company or their employer) you are likely to have to issue an invoice in order to get paid. If you do not get paid at the time of the treatment you need to keep track of who owes you money, so that you do collect eventually. I include a separate debtor column in my analysis book so I don't forget.

Banking

You should keep your business bank account separate from your own personal banking. This is so that your personal and business lives are kept separate. It also makes it easier to track payments in and out and agree them with your accounts. If HMRC want to check your business tax affairs they will usually ask to see your bank statements.

You may not want them to start asking questions about your payments to supermarkets, clothing stores or money which you have received from family or friends, such as birthday presents.

Unlike personal banking which is currently provided free, banks usually charge fees for business bank accounts. These may be a monthly fee and/or a fee for each cheque or credit processed. You may be able to find a bank which offers free business banking for a period, but ultimately you will be charged and the interest which you will earn on any cash in the account will most likely be much lower than a personal account. Those who prefer internet banking can usually arrange this on most business accounts.

Once you have chosen and set up your business bank account, it is better to bank all money earned, cash as well as cheques, even if you then need to withdraw money as a separate transaction. Cash is otherwise untraceable. By paying it all in you can correlate your income with your diary. Don't be tempted to 'lose' payments in cash. It is far better to be legal and above board in your financial affairs. Cash businesses are more prone to close scrutiny by HMRC.

Similarly, all business expenses should be paid out of this account rather than from your personal bank account. If you take any money or other assets (e.g. some vitamin supplements which you normally sell to your customers) out of the business for your own use you have to show this in your accounts as 'drawings'. In the case of the vitamin supplements you have to show the amount of the drawings as the amount at which you would sell the goods to your customers, i.e. your business makes a profit selling the goods to you. Although it can seem cumbersome, it does make the overall process of keeping and checking your accounts much easier.

Keep all copies of bank statements, paying in books and cheque stubs in a safe place, in case they are requested by HMRC.

Although banks will supply copies of bank statements on request they usually charge for this. Paying in books cannot be replaced and are a vital link between your bank details and the income recorded in your analysis book.

ANNUAL ACCOUNTS

Each year you will have to produce a summary of your income and expenditure in order to produce a record of your profit or loss for the year and the assets used in the business. You can decide what date you are going to use as your year end. Popular dates are 31 December to tie in with the calendar or 31 March which more or less coincides with the tax year. You can, however, choose the date which suits you best. Once decided though, you are likely to use this for every year thereafter as it is very messy to change your accounting date.

Depending on your own skills and interest you may wish to find an accountant who specialises in dealing with small businesses to help with this stage. Most charge by the hour (my accountant jokes that it's actually by the minute!), so you will reduce the cost if you have kept your own books on a regular basis and retained all the supporting documents listed above.

Most of the information will come straight from your analysis book. However, it may have to be adjusted for any expenses which you have incurred before the year end but not yet paid (known as accruals) and any amounts which you have paid but some of the payment will cover a later period (known as prepayments). For example, you may have rented a room from a clinic just before your year end but not received the invoice. You would therefore accrue for this cost at the normal room rate. Equally, you may have paid your annual professional membership fee but it still has nine months to run. Three quarters of the membership benefit will therefore arise next year and so that proportion of the fee should be shown as a prepayment.

The aim is to make sure that only the expenses incurred in order to earn the income are set against that income in order to calculate the profit. An illustrative income and expenditure account is set out in Appendix 3.

Once you know your profit you can then go on to look at taxation. The following is merely a summary of the main principles. You will almost certainly need advice in this area and should seek the assistance of your accountant.

INCOME TAX

As I said before, if you are working for an employer, they should automatically deduct tax at source under the Pay as You Earn (PAYE) scheme. Your employer will send you an annual summary of your income and tax deducted using a form P60 which you should keep.

SELF EMPLOYMENT

You must notify your local Tax Office within three months of starting your business using form CWF1. If you don't, you may incur a penalty. Once you have notified HMRC they will then issue you with a Tax Return shortly after each 5 April. Self employed individuals and partners are required to complete a Tax Return for each year. You must submit it by 31 October if you submit a paper copy, or by 31 January in the following year if you submit your return online over the internet. It is important that you submit your Return by the appropriate date if you wish to avoid an automatic £100 penalty. If you submit your Tax Return by 31 October HMRC will calculate the amount of tax that you owe. Otherwise you will get an online calculation after you have completed your Return over the internet.

For historic reasons the tax year runs from 6 April to 5 April, even if you have chosen a different date as your year end. Your income tax liability for the tax year will normally be based on the profits earned by your business in the accounts that end in the tax year. For example, a Tax Return for 2009/10 is normally based on the profits for the year ended 31 December 2009 where that is the date to which the business makes up its annual accounts. However, special rules will apply in the early years of starting your business.

If your gross income is less than an amount set out by HMRC* you need only submit a summary of your profits. Where they are more than that, more detailed accounts are required. In either case, your tax liability will be based on the accounts which you have prepared as above.

At this stage some expenditure will not be allowed as a deduction for tax purposes, though needless to say, all of your income will be taxed! You won't be able to claim a deduction for expenditure incurred entertaining professional contacts or suppliers over lunch. Nor can you claim for expenditure on clothing where you might normally expect to wear that clothing when not at work. However, if you wear a uniform or tunic then this may be allowable. My clothes tend to become marked by oil when I give massage so I claim a tax deduction for them as I could not wear them for any other purpose. They are, in effect, a cost of being a therapist.

In addition, where you spend money on something which will last you a long time such as a couch, other professional equipment or a computer you may not get a deduction immediately. Instead, the tax system allows you to claim a capital allowance for this

* See Appendix 4 for key rates and reliefs announced before 31 March 2009

equipment each year. Expenditure up to the Annual Investment Allowance* will qualify for a full deduction in the first year which will cover most small businesses. Expenditure above this amount may still qualify for plant and machinery allowances*. As these allowances are deducted on what is known as the reducing balance (the residual cost after all the allowances have been deducted for earlier years), this can mean that the tax deduction is spread over many years.

If you are working from home you may also be able to claim a proportion of:

- your household fuel bills for heat, light and laundry
- your telephone /mobile phone call costs where it is not a dedicated business line

As a self employed person you can also claim a deduction for expenses if you use your car for home visits. This differs from an employee who is unable to claim a deduction for their travel costs between their home and their normal place of work. In theory, you could work out an actual cost per mile of driving your car and then claim that amount for every mile driven on business. In practice, most people use an Approved Mileage Allowance* which is published by HMRC.

You should by now have a figure for your taxable profit for the year. From this you can deduct your personal allowance* and any contributions you have made to a pension scheme. Amounts remaining will then be taxed at the rates set by the Government. The rates of tax for 2008/9 are set out in Appendix 4 with some

* See Appendix 4 for key rates and reliefs announced before 31 March 2009

provisional figures for 2009/2010. The final 2009/2010 figures and those for later years will be available from my website.

Unlike the system for employees where tax is deducted from their pay packet each week/month, the self-employed practitioner pays tax in two equal instalments on 31 July and 31 January each year. It is vital to plan carefully to make sure that you have the cash available as interest will be incurred on any tax which is paid late. The instalments will be based on the profits which you made in the previous year and the balance is payable on the following 31 January.

For example, Sam reported his taxable income as £10,000 in the year ended 5 April 2008 and had tax of £2,000 to pay. He will therefore pay an instalment of £1,000 for the tax year (ending 5 April 2009) on 31 January 2009 and £1,000 on 31 July 2009. If the profits of his business have increased, Sam will pay any additional tax on his 2008/09 profits (after deducting the instalment payments) on 31 January 2010.

If Sam's profits had fallen, it would be worth him applying for the instalment payment to be reduced. This can be done using form SA303, available from your Tax Office or online from HMRC.

NATIONAL INSURANCE

Having contacted HMRC to inform them you are starting a business, you will also have to complete form CWF1 in order to organise your National Insurance contributions. If your income from self employment exceeds an amount set by HMRC* you are obliged to pay a Class 2 stamp at a fixed rate per week*. These can be paid by monthly Direct Debit. You will also have to pay a

* See Appendix 4 for key rates and reliefs announced before 31 March 2009

Class 4 stamp* to the extent that your income exceeds the annual exemption*. This is paid with your income tax liability in July and January each year.

These payments entitle you to basic sickness pay, maternity pay, and your state pension. The payments from these are not large, so you may well wish to insure yourself separately against the risk of being unable to work and make payments into a personal pension scheme for your retirement. There is more about insurance in Chapter 1.

CORPORATION TAX

If you decide to carry on your business through a company you will pay corporation tax rather than income tax. The basic calculation of your taxable profit is completed in substantially the same way as it is for income tax. You should, however, get a tax deduction for amounts which you pay yourself by way of salary, although the salary itself will be subject to tax under PAYE. In addition, you will get no personal allowance on the company profits, and the rates of tax are likely to be higher for most small businesses.

VALUE ADDED TAX

If your total annual sales income exceeds (or is expected to exceed) the registration limit* you must register for VAT. Thereafter your fees are likely to be subject to VAT at the standard rate*. You will have to charge this to your clients and pay it over to HMRC, although you will be able to reclaim any VAT which you are charged on goods and services received as part of your business. There are a number of exceptions to this rule, most notably

* See Appendix 4 for key rates and reliefs announced before 31 March 2009

registered osteopaths and chiropractors, who are exempt from charging VAT on their provision of medical care.

I conclude this section in the same way that I started. Taxation is a complex area which could and does fill many books in its own right; I have only given a basic introduction. It is an area where you will probably need some professional help to set you on the right road.

CHECKLIST

❏   have you informed HMRC that you have started a business?

❏   have you sorted out your National Insurance contributions?

❏   have you formulated a way of keeping financial records?

❏   have you chosen a date for your year end?

❏   have you opened a business bank account?

❏   have you found yourself an accountant?

12 THE FUTURE FOR COMPLEMENTARY THERAPIES IN THE UK

The best thing about the future is that it comes one day at a time.
ABRAHAM LINCOLN

REGULATION AND YOU

At present, regulation and registration of complementary therapists in the UK is voluntary. This means that there are no laws to protect the public from unscrupulous, unqualified, abusive or incompetent therapists. While we ourselves work for the highest good of our clients, this lack of regulation impacts on how complementary therapists are viewed as professionals by both the public seeking treatments and by other professionals. At the very minimum, after you've done all that training, it would be nice if the public could tell the difference between you and an impostor, wouldn't it?

For the past 10 years, the various therapy associations have been working to agree standards of training, practice, and requirements for each complementary therapy and to set up a national register. The aim of this is to help protect the public, and ensures that regulation of practitioners is carried out by the regulatory bodies, while supporting them is the role of the professional organisations (umbrella groups). The long-term aim is that many therapies will eventually come under statutory regulation – regulation by law. Osteopaths and chiropractors have already led the way. Initially regulating their practitioners voluntarily, they are now regulated by law, meaning that they and their clients/patients are legally protected. Today, no one can call themselves an 'osteopath' or 'chiropractor' without having undertaken recognised training, having their name on a central register, and keeping up to date with developments in their field.

Other therapies are now following on their heels, putting robust measures in place for self regulation as a step on the road towards full statutory regulation. Through adopting good business practices and by delivering excellent professional standards these other therapies may, in the longer term, also find themselves ready for statutory regulation. That should go a long way to bringing about greater credibility and respect for complementary therapists as a whole. And that, in turn, should mean better business for all of us, so it makes sense to do what you can now to prepare yourself.

None of the three organisations listed below cover all therapies and each has its own register. You will need to check which would be the most appropriate one for you. Your training school may well be able to advise you.

The three regulatory bodies for complementary therapists, each (at present) covering different therapies are:

●   The Complementary and Natural Healthcare Council (CNHC)
●   The General Regulatory Council for Complementary Therapies (GRCCT)
●   The British Complementary Therapies Council for Voluntary Self Regulation (BCTC)

The Council for Healthcare Regulatory Excellence (CHRE) oversees the regulation of chiropractors, osteopaths, dentists, doctors, paramedics, pharmacists, nurses and midwives, physiotherapists and optometrists. There is also a website, Health Professional Check, which anyone can use to check whether a health professional in the above is listed.

The Complementary and Natural Healthcare Council

The CNHC was established in April 2008 with government backing from the Department of Health. It was facilitated by the Prince's Foundation for Integrated Health. It is now a separate independent organisation whose key function is to enhance protection of the public. CNHC hope that 'Registered with CNHC' will become recognised as the hallmark of quality.

From mid-January 2009, the CNHC will accept applications to the register from massage and nutritional therapists. It is expected that more therapies will be added in due course.

The General Regulatory Council for Complementary Therapies

The GRCCT is establishing a national register of therapists. Again, not all therapies are able to register with them at present. The GRCCT also provides a complaints procedure and has the power to remove a practitioner from the national register in the event of a serious complaint being upheld.

British Complementary Therapies Council for Voluntary Self Regulation

The BCTCVSR has 20 member therapies. It is expected that more therapies will be added.

These regulatory organisations recognise the value and importance of each other. They also cooperate to ensure that if a therapist is removed from the register of one organisation, they will be unable to join another.

The regulatory organisations say they will:

- give you greater credibility and higher professional standing
- provide access to CPD
- provide a route for enquiries about complementary practitioners

And that they will give your clients:

- the assurance of high standards
- an appropriate complaints procedure
- a hallmark for quality

Contact details for all the above are in Appendix 5.

13 PLANNING YOUR FUTURE AND MOVING ON

The riders in a race do not stop when they reach the goal. There is a little finishing canter before coming to a standstill. There is time to hear the kind voices of friends, and say to oneself 'The work is done.' OLIVER WENDELL HOLMES JNR

If you have taken on board all the advice in this book, you will be well on your way to a satisfying successful career as a therapist. But you won't be able to sit on your laurels and think that you've 'got there.' A healthy practice will grow and change over time. It may be that you will want to continue just as you are, but it is important that you plan to do that rather than drift along: you'll need to evaluate your achievements to date and plan your future goals.

In reality, many of us continue to practise our therapy while also teaching or writing or whatever. After some years in practice you may wish to pass on your expertise and experience (as we have done in this book). You may also find that as you grow older you no longer have quite the same energy levels, but you still need to earn a living. It is worth considering options that are less physically demanding, while allowing you to remain within your profession.

- have you achieved what you set out to do?
- how could you improve things further?
- how would you like to progress?
- where do you see yourself next year, in 5 or 10 years?
- will you continue as you are?
- will you teach, write or lecture?
- will you make and/or sell associated products?

Moving on

If you are just starting out as a therapist it may seem odd to be thinking about when you no longer wish to continue, for whatever reason. But when the time approaches, it is important to plan a good exit strategy. You are not working in your clients' best interests by just stopping, leaving them high and dry. At the very least, you should inform your entire client base that you intend to stop working and preferably try to find other practitioners who would take on extra clients. Don't underestimate the loyalty you have built up. A client called me recently for an appointment and I hadn't seen her for 17 years! She still regarded me as 'her' therapist.

Consider whether you might sell your client list or your entire practice to someone. Think about what you have of value that could provide some income for you. If you have given your all to your practice, it is only right that you should reap the benefit from all that investment as fully as possible when you choose to stop.

Selling your entire business would mean selling your client list, premises (if you have any), and tangible stock (couches, oils, towels, and other equipment) and intangibles (intellectual property). If you intend to sell up in this way, obtain a valuation on your business first – you don't want to sell yourself short! A solicitor, or estate agent or chartered surveyor (if you have premises) should be able to do this. It may also be the case that your business is worth more broken up than as a whole. Engage a solicitor to help you and to draw up the paperwork to make sure there are no hitches.

Perhaps you don't think it's worth the hassle? Reconsider. How many regular clients do you have? How much have they been worth to you over the years? If you simply stop practising and don't sell, those clients will go and find another therapist anyway. You'll be giving your clients away for nothing when you could be getting several hundreds or possibly even thousands of pounds for them, depending on how well established you are!

Think about how attractive an established client list would currently be to you, for example. If someone offered you a list right now of 20 clients worth about £20K a year to you, would you be interested? Yes, you'd have to find the upfront cost of say £5–10K, depending on what else the purchase of the business includes, but the earnings potential is so good that it's surely a highly appealing thought. And that is exactly what you should think about cashing in on when you feel your days of practising are coming to an end. Remember – you've earned it!

AND FINALLY . . .

Whatever the challenges and ups and downs of your life are, remember that you are privileged to be able to work as a therapist. This book was written with the aim of helping you achieve professional success balanced with caring responsibly for your clients. **Here's to success!**

Appendix 1

David's Projected Business Costs

Couch	£1,250
Expected replacement period of couch	5 years

	£
Annual proportion of capital replacement cost	250
Professional indemnity insurance	150
Professional subscriptions	100
Annual training courses	250
Advertisement in phone book	100
Total annual fixed costs	**850**
Clinic rental cost per client	11
Paper towels/wipes/oils	1
Bottle of water per client	1
Travel costs	2
Variable costs	**15**

Notes (see table opposite):

1. The breakeven point is where David's total annual income equals (or first exceeds) his total annual costs of treating that number of clients

2. With fixed costs of £850 per year, David has to treat 170 clients per year to break even if he charges £20 per client reducing to 25 clients if he charges £50 per client

3. David's variable travel costs may reduce if he is able to treat more than one client in each visit to the clinic. This possibility is likely to increase the more clients he treats, but it would require more complex modelling than is practical. When starting out keep things as simple as possible.

Calculating the breakeven point

Number of clients per year	ANNUAL COSTS			ANNUAL INCOME			
	Fixed £	Variable £	Total £	£20 per client £	£30 per client £	£40 per client £	£50 per client £
10	850	150	1000	200	300	400	500
20	850	300	1150	400	600	800	1000
25	850	375	1225	500	750	1000	1250
30	850	450	1300	600	900	1200	1500
34	850	510	1360	680	1020	1360	1700
40	850	600	1450	800	1200	1600	2000
50	850	750	1600	1000	1500	2000	2500
57	850	855	1705	1140	1710	2280	2850
60	850	900	1750	1200	1800	2400	3000
100	850	1500	2350	2000	3000	4000	5000
150	850	2250	3100	3000	4500	6000	7500
160	850	2400	3250	3200	4800	6400	8000
170	850	2550	3400	3400	5100	6800	8500
180	850	2700	3550	3600	5400	7200	9000
190	850	2850	3700	3800	5700	7600	9500
200	850	3000	3850	4000	6000	8000	10000

Appendix 2

INCOME AND EXPENDITURE YEAR ENDED 31 DECEMBER 20XX

				INCOME		
Date	Cheque £	Cash £	Debtor £	Name	**Ref**	Total £
2-Jan	40.00			Smith		40.00
2-Jan	40.00			Jones		40.00
2-Jan			40.00	Griffiths		40.00
3-Jan		40.00		Singh		40.00
4-Jan	40.00			Harris		40.00
7-Jan			40.00	Scott		40.00
9-Jan	40.00		(40.00)	Griffiths		0.00
10-Jan				Towel Supplier	**0901**	(17.50)
10-Jan				Yellow Pages	**0902**	(125.00)
12-Jan				Supermaket chain	**0903**	(2.50)
14-Jan				Office Supplier	**0904**	(70.00)
	160.00	40.00	40.00		240.00	25.00

Notes

1. Income has been split between the amounts received in cash, that by cheque and also any debtors. This helps to check the amounts paid into the business bank account

2. Griffiths was originally a debtor, but paid by cheque on 9 January. Both these events are shown as separate transactions so that I can see who still owes me money. In this case Scott still owes for his treatment.

3. The shaded column in the middle of the page is calculated automatically and keeps a running total of all of the income and expenditure. On these figures I have made a cash surplus of £25 in the period.

EXPENDITURE (categories as appropriate)					
Paper towels £	Adverts £	Water £	Clothing £	Sundry Expenditure £	Description
17.50					
	125.00				
				2.50	Tea light candles
				70.00	Filing cabinet
17.50	125.00	0.00	0.00	72.50	

4. I have included a reference for each of the items of expenditure so that I can match this up with an invoice in my files

5. Expenditure has been shown in an approropiate expense column for my business. Only a few examples are included here. However, you should choose the main types of expenditure you incur regularly in your business. Small items or irregular items of expenditure have been included in a miscellaneous column with a brief description of the cost in the column next to it

APPENDIX 3

INCOME AND EXPENDITURE YEAR ENDED 31 DECEMBER 20XX

	£	£
Income		12,245

Expenditure

Paper towels	50	
Water	307	
Massage oils	107	
Advertising	125	
Clothing	63	
Professional Insurance	150	
Subscriptions/journals	80	
Training received	195	
Publications/books	41	
Printing/stationery	84	
Business telephone	234	
Motor costs	226	
Travel + subsistence	92	
Sundry - repairs	48	
Sundry - plants / flowers	21	
Sundry - incense	14	
Sundry - candles	12	

			1,849
			10,396

		Total £	Business £
Gas	10%	600	60
Electricity	15%	750	113
			(173)

Profit for the year	10,223

Notes:

1. The accounts show the total income and expenditure for the year from the business. It adds up all of the individual items of income and expenditure from your analysis sheets to show the summary for the year.

2. Where you spend money mostly for domestic purposes but also partly for business, the costs will not normally be included in your business analysis sheets. Each year you should estimate the percentage of any household costs incurred specifically for business purposes as accurately as possible such as the gas or electricity spent heating or lighting a room which you use to treat clients. Here we have calculated that 10% of our gas bill and 15 % of the electricity bill is down to business use.

Appendix 4

KEY UK TAXATION RATES AND ALLOWANCES

	2008/09		2009/10 Provisional (subject to Budget and enactment)	
Income Tax				
Simplified Accounts with tax return turnover below	per year	£64,000	per year	£64,000
Annual Personal Allowance		£6,035		£6,475
Basic rate	20%	Up to £34,800	20%	Up to £37,400
Higher rate	40%	Above £34,800	40%	Above £37,400
National Insurance				
Class 2 contributions	per week	£2.30	per week	£2.40
Small earnings exemption	per year	£4,825		£5,075
Class 4 contributions				
Lower profit limit (LPL)	per year	£5,435		£5,715
Upper profit limit (UPL)	per year	£40,040		£43,875
Rates				
below LPL		0%		0%
between LPL and UPL		8%		8%
above UPL		1%		1%
Approved Mileage Allowance				
Up to 10,000 miles	per mile	40p	per mile	40p
Over 10,000 miles	per mile	25p	per mile	25p
Corporation Tax				
Profit less than £300,000		21%		21%
Capital Allowances				
Annual Investment Allowance	per year	£50,000	per year	£50,000
Plant and machinery allowance	per year, reducing balance	20%	per year, reducing balance	20%
Value Added Tax				
General rate	15% to 1 January 2010		17.5% from 1 January 2010	
Registration limit - turnover above	per year	£67,000	per year	£67,000

Useful contacts

The authors
Celia Johnson www.successful therapist.co.uk
Helen Parkins www.helenparkins.co.uk

Regulatory organisations
Complementary and Natural Healthcare Council
0845 121 1929 www.cnhc.org.uk

British Complementary Therapies Council
for Voluntary Self Regulation
www.bctcvsr.org.uk

General Regulatory Council for Complementary Therapies
0870 3144031 www.grcct.org

Council for Healthcare Regulatory Excellence www.chre.org.uk

Health Professionals Check www.hpc-uk.org

Professional organisations
There are many more professional organisations than space to
list them here. This is a small selection.

Massage Training Institute www.massagetraining.co.uk

Federation of Holistic Therapists www.fht.org.uk

International Federation of Professional Aromatherapists www.
ifparoma.org

International Federation of Aromatherapists www.ifaroma.org

Association of Reflexologists www.aor.org.uk

General Council for Massage Therapy www.gcmt.org.uk

Complementary Medicine Association www.the-cma.org.uk

British Complementary Medicine Association www.bcma.co.uk

Aromatherapy Council www.aromatherapycouncil.co.uk

Prince of Wales Foundation www.fih.org.uk

Manual Lymphatic Drainage www.mlduk.org.uk

GOVERNMENT ORGANISATIONS
Health and Safety Executive www.hse.gov.uk

RIDDOR www.hse.gov.uk/riddor

Data Protection www.dpr.gov.uk www.ico.gov.uk

Her Majesty's Revenue and Customs www.hmrc.gov.uk

Business Link www.businesslink.gov.uk

WEBSITE DESIGN AND MANAGEMENT
www.webhealer.com 0870 757 9878

www.brand-you.co.uk 020 8123 0802

WITNESS
professional boundaries charity   020 7922 7800
www.professionalboundaries.org.uk

LIFE AND BUSINESS COACHING
Rasheed Ogunlaru www.rasaru.com

MARKETING
Steven Harold www.marketingtherapists.com

FINANCIAL AND BUSINESS ADVICE
Heather Darnell www.ask-the-boss.co.uk

NETWORKING AND ONLINE DIRECTORIES
www.networking4therapists.com

www.healers.co.uk

www.embodyforyou.com

PR AND BRANDING
Paula Gardner www.doyourownpr.com

Edge Communications marinajarnold @aol.com 07702 203915

OILS AND EQUIPMENT
Essential oils and carrier oils
Shirley Price Aromatherapy 01455 615054
www.shirleyprice.com

Fleur Aromatherapy   01608 658816 www.fleur.co.uk

Essentially Oils 0845 130 4400 www.essentiallyoils.com

Absolute Aromas 01420 540400 www.absolute-aromas.com

Aromatherapy Associates 020 8569 7030
www.aromatherapyassociates.com

Waxes
Tui Waxes 01749 860387 www.songbirdnaturals.co.uk

Couches
Plinth 2000 01449 767887 www.plinth2000.com (hydraulic couches)

Therapy Essentials 0800 083 5530 www.therapyessentials.co.uk

Marshcouch 01442 263199 www.marshcouch.com

The Massage Table Store 01827 60013 www.massagetablestore.com

Covers, towels, couch rolls and accessories
Tavy Covers 01752 839222 www.tavycovers.com

Majestic Towels 0121 772 0936 www.majestictowels.co.uk

Osteopathic Supplies Limited 01432 263939 www.o-s-l.com

Homeopathic supplies
Weleda UK 0115 944 8210 www.weleda.co.uk

Ainsworth's Homeopathic Pharmacy 0201 7935 5330
www.ainsworths.com

Clothing
DK Profashion 0800 0329976 www.dk-profashion.co.uk

Alexanders 0117 959 4444 www.alexanderleisure.co.uk

BOOKS AND JOURNALS
Cygnus books 01550 777701 www.cygnus-books.co.uk

The Tao of Books 01379 676000 www.taobook.com

What Doctors Don't Tell You www.wddty.co.uk

Massage World 020 7387 9111 www.massageworld.co.uk

Positive Health (now online only) www.positivehealth.com

CAM magazine www.cam-mag.com

Leon Chaitow www.leonchaitow.com

INSURANCE
Three Counties Insurance Brokers Ltd (Insurance Data Services) 01789 293815 www.3co.co.uk

Balens 01684 580771 www.balens.co.uk

Therapy Insurance Services 023 8062 1550 (affiliated to FHT)

Alan Boswell 01603 218000 www.alanboswell.com

Index